What the Plus!

Google+ for the Rest of Us

GUY KAWASAKI

Mc
Graw
Hill

NEW YORK   CHICAGO   SAN FRANCISCO
LISBON   LONDON   MADRID   MEXICO CITY   MILAN
NEW DELHI   SAN JUAN   SEOUL   SINGAPORE
SYDNEY   TORONTO

The *McGraw·Hill* Companies

1 2 3 4 5 6 7 8 9 0   QFR/QFR   1 8 7 6 5 4 3 2

ISBN 978-0-07-181010-4
MHID   0-07-181010-2

Design by Mauna Eichner and Lee Fukui

McGraw-Hill books are available at special quantity discounts to use as premiums and sales promotions, or for use in corporate training programs. To contact a representative please e-mail us at bulksales@mcgraw-hill.com.

This book is printed on acid-free paper.

Contents

Preface

> *Never ask what sort of computer a guy drives. If he's*
> *a Mac user, he'll tell you. If not, why embarrass him?*
>
> TOM CLANCY

Six years ago, you probably would not have joined Facebook—if you even knew what Facebook was. Ditto for Twitter. Today, you're probably using at least one of the services if you're reading this book. Both services, to use Malcolm Gladwell's term, "tipped."

Do you remember when everyone predicted that Myspace would control the world? Today, its traffic is a rounding error. Myspace didn't tip. It imploded. Things change. Rapidly. Unexpectedly. Unbelievably.

Will Google+ do a Facebook or do a Myspace? My prediction is that Google+ will not only tip, but it will exceed Facebook and Twitter. That said, the first time I shared a post, no one responded or commented. I shared another post, and again nothing happened.

After a few days, I circled ("friended" and "liked" in Facebook-speak and "followed" in Twitter-speak) two dozen people, and I received a handful of responses to my posts. Still, Google+ was a ghost town compared to Facebook and Twitter. Why was my buddy Robert Scoble beaming about the wonderfulness of Google+? I was dumbfounded—what was I missing?

Then I figured out that only people whom I had circled could see my posts. When I started sharing publicly, I received dozens of comments, and all goodness broke loose. Compared to Twitter and Facebook, Google+ comments came in quicker, slicker, and thicker.

The clouds parted, and Google+ enchanted me. I reduced my activity on Facebook and Twitter, and Google+ became my social operating system. However, many people, particularly pundits, did not (and still don't) share my passion for Google+. After initially writing positive reviews, many of them predicted Google+'s demise.

On the home front, I tried to get my wife and two teenagers to use Google+, but the service didn't stick for them because (a) my wife has no time for any social networking at all and (b) my sons' friends weren't on Google+.

My experience as an Apple evangelist flashed before my eyes: Macintosh was a better computer, and many people didn't "get it." Now, Google+ is a better social network, and many people don't get it, either.

> *Isn't it about time the Macintosh was simply discontinued—put down like an old dog?*
> JOHN DVORAK, *PC Magazine*, June 17, 2002

> *It* [Google+] *may not be dead, and it's entirely possible I'm shoveling dirt on something that's still writhing around, promising me it is in fact the next big thing, but I'm now deaf to its cries.*
> PAUL TASSI, *Forbes*, August 15, 2011

From my perspective, Google+ is to Facebook and Twitter what Macintosh is to Windows: better, but fewer people use it, and the pundits prophesy that it will fail. As a lover of great products, this rankles my soul.

I hate when people don't use the best tool. Sometimes people don't know that a better tool exists. Sometimes they know it exists but not that it's better. Sometimes they try the better tool, but the tool doesn't stick for them.

The year 1987 was the last time I wrote a book about a product (*The Macintosh Way*). After using Google+ for a few months, I felt the need to write another product-oriented book. This book explains **"what the plus"** makes Google+ as special as Macintosh.

My goals are to help you to derive as much joy and value from Google+ as I do and that we can make Google+ tip.

Acknowledgments

> *We've heard that a million monkeys at a million keyboards could produce the complete works of Shakespeare; now, thanks to the Internet, we know that is not true.*
>
> Robert Wilensky

Halley Suitt Tucker is the mother of *What the Plus!* because she convinced me to write and self-publish it during a dinner in Boston. Along the way, these folks also performed mid-wife magic:

- **Content:** Fraser Cain, Marylene Delbourg-Delphis, Malaika Frijimersum, Michael Hermeston, Bradley Horowitz, Bill Meade, Jaana Nyström, and Katie Watson.

- **Contribution:** Peg Fitzpatrick, Dave Powell, and Lynette Young.

- **Construction:** Rachelle Mandik copyedited this book. Then Shawn Welch designed and produced it. Ana Frazao designed the cover. Chris Howard, Will Mayall, Karen Minster, Gina Poss, and Derek Scott also helped get it out the door.

Near the end of the writing process, I asked my closest 1.1 million friends on Google+ if they'd like to test this book. Approximately 240 people responded, and I sent the manuscript to them. Within a week, approximately 100 people provided their feedback. They found 147 typos and twenty-seven factual errors as well as showed me sixty-seven ways to improve the book. (I counted duplicates of advice only once.)

These are the members of the beta-test team:

Michele Abraham, Matt Acuff, Zach Alcorn, Jeff Angcanan, Terry Babij, Jennifer Bailey, Mike Bainbridge, Leonardo Benveniste, Lici Beveridge, Paul Biedermann, Jan Borgwardt, Darla Brown, Tim Burrows, Roland Byrd, Pat Byrne, Matt Campbell, Arjun Chandrappa, Jonathan Chu, Katie Clark, Marlies Cohen, Michael Cunningham, Kenken Clarin, Robert Coller, John Daddow, Kishore Dandu, Jerry M. Denman, Ben Diaz, Tim Dippel, Jeff Dorchester, Tracey Edgar, Jon Elbery, Brandy Ellis, Connie Feil, Bryan Fuselier, John Gallagher, Sriram Gopalan, Greg Gorman, J. H. Grace, Matt Gray, Terrie Gray, Jon Greer, Dawn Groves, Gustavo Guiomar, Hakan Gül, Jose Hanchi, Jophn Heckendorn, Siddhartha Herdegen, Dave Hidding, Adam Howard, Kim Josephs, Jeremie Kanter, Jennifer Karr, Josh Keene, Scott Knaster, Remo Kommnick, Kimberly Lau, Gary Lee, Ken Lee, Steven Lowe, Allison Makowski, Dusko Maksimovic, Daniel Mandel, Didier J. Mary, Chrisann Merriman, Linda Michels, Allen Moran, Rollin Morris, Marc Myton, Nasir Naeem, Chetan Naik, Claudia Neumann, Brandon Odegard, Gary Oppenhuis, Dan O'Shea, Frank Ouimette, Yashdeep Patil, Jessica Pierce, Katherine Pereira, Crystal Ponti, Peter Prescot, Tzafrir Rehan, Neil Roberts, Paul Roustan, Silvino Pires dos Santos, Daiva Rackauskiene, Jacqueline Samoise, Jeff Schultz, Josef Siewruk, Bob Soltys, Martha Spelman, Keith Spiro, Patrick Stainier, Tara Stuttler, Jirapong Supasaovapak, Thomas Tenkely, Chet Thaker, David Thomas, Hal Thompson, Pat Toal, Alvin Toro, Pablo Valcárcel, Gideon van der Westhuysen, Danielle Violot, Lisa Kalner Williams, Scott Yates, Aygul Zagidullina, and Keivan Zolfaghari.

Why I Love Google+

> *Life is a process of becoming, a combination of*
> *states we have to go through. Where people fail is*
> *that they wish to elect a state and remain in it.*
> *This is a kind of death.*
>
> ANAÏS NIN, *Winter of Artifice*

YET ANOTHER SOCIAL-MEDIA PLATFORM

More than 1,000,000 people follow me on Twitter, and 250,000 people subscribe to my Facebook account, so I'm not a newbie to social media. Like many people, I need another social-media service like I need more e-mail or my dog to throw up on my carpet.

And yet I jumped on Google+ (after I figured out how to publicly share posts, anyway). I spend two hours a day on Google+ because it's enjoyable and good for my brand as a writer, speaker, and startup-company advisor. Or, more truthfully, Google+ is so enjoyable that I rationalize that it's good for my brand.

My Twitter stats: really, I'm not a newbie to social media.

In addition to my fondness for its members and their comments, Google+ embodies many appealing attributes that make social networking better. Here's how Google+,

Facebook, Twitter, and Pinterest compare along some parameters that are important to me:

	Google+	Facebook	Twitter	Pinterest
Post size limit	100,000 characters	63,206 characters	140 characters	500 characters
Profile	One profile photo, one to five picture photos area displayed at once, multiple text fields	One large profile photo, one smaller inset profile photo, and multiple text fields	One small profile photo and 160 characters	One profile photo, 200 characters, multiple text fields
Video conferencing	Yes, 10 people total, unlimited watch-and-listen only guests	One-to-one only	No	No
Visibility of posts	Any follower as well as the public	"Edgerank" determines which friends and fans can see your posts	Any follower as well as the public	Any follower as well as the public
After-the-fact editing of posts	Yes	Sometimes, if you edit within seconds of posting	No	Yes
After-the-fact editing of comments	Yes	Yes	No	Yes
Grouping posts with comments and responses	Yes	Yes	Not really, unless you are willing to search through every @ mention	Yes
Display of photos in posts	Yes	Yes, but smaller in size unless you choose to "feature" it	No, reader must click on a link	Yes
Display photo albums in posts	Yes	Yes, but probably 80% as good as Google+'s, contain ads	No	No

Google+, Facebook, Twitter, and Pinterest are in a constant features race, so this chart is ever-changing. However, it shows a trend: Google+ has powerful and sophisticated features that the competition doesn't, and Google+ does things in ways that make more sense to me.

For example, did you know that all your friends and followers on Facebook cannot see your updates? This Facebook "Insights" report shows that only 6,799 of the 33,754 fans of my *Enchantment* book page (www.facebook.com/enchantment) could have seen my updates. (Some studies indicate that only 12 percent of one's buddies on Facebook can see your updates.) By contrast, *100* percent of my followers on Google+ can see what I post there.

Also, Facebook groups individual photos from separate posts and makes them into one post. For example, during a visit to the University of Oregon, I posted three photos over an eight-hour period. Each post was separate, and Facebook decided to glom them together as the illustration on page 4 shows. If I wanted them together, I would have made an album. I wanted separate posts.

Facebook Insights report.

Google+ would win if Facebook and Twitter launched today. However, Facebook and Twitter started more than five years before Google+, and they amassed large customer bases before Google+ entered the market. A good analogy is that people don't enjoy a small party (Google+) where they don't know anyone, compared to a big party (Facebook and Twitter) where they know lots of people.

My counterargument is that it's your own fault if you don't have a good time at a small party where there are many beautiful and interesting people.

Facebook decided to put together three pictures from three separate posts.

RATIONAL EXUBERANCE

If Google+ was "two guys/gals in a garage with seed funding," I would adopt a wait-and-see attitude, but this is hardly the case. Although new projects have failed at Google before (as at many large companies), this doesn't mean that search is the only thing Google can do.

> *Google+ is Google itself. We're extending it across all that we do—search, ads, Chrome, Android, Maps, YouTube—so that each of those services contributes to our understanding of who you are.*
>
> BRADLEY HOROWITZ, vice president, products for Google+, Google. *Wired,* September 27, 2011

As my mother used to say, "Some things need to be believed to be seen," so here is why I believe in Google+ before

I've seen 800 million people (the number that Facebook bandies about) get on it:

- **Google has a track record.** Google has delivered better mousetraps when most people didn't think better mousetraps were necessary. For example, Yahoo!, Inktomi, and AltaVista were good enough for searching, and Hotmail was good enough for e-mail. Google's record isn't flawless, but no company's is— even Apple had the Apple III, LISA, Newton, and Macintosh Office.

- **Google is dead serious about this business.** Insiders tell me Google+ is one of the top priorities of Google. It's not an experiment or project buried within another business unit. The guy who runs Google+, Vic Gundotra, reports directly to Larry Page, the CEO of Google. Google+ is a core part of the functionality of all of Google, and it would be astoundingly embarrassing for Google+ to fail.

- **Google has infinite money and talent.** Having infinite money and talent doesn't mean an organization is infallible, as Webvan ($1.2 billion invested so people could order asparagus online), Lehman Brothers, and Enron have proven. But having infinite money and talent doesn't guarantee you'll fail, either. Google is assaulting two big companies on their established turfs, so money and talent are necessary in this battle.

- **Google owns the river.** In ancient lore, one of the labors given to Hercules was to clean the huge Augean stables in a day. Hercules accomplished this herculean task by diverting the Alpheus and

Peneus Rivers through the stables. Google owns one of the biggest rivers of Internet traffic (search), and it can divert people to Google+ anytime it wants. For example, when Google put an arrow on its search page pointing to the button to click to join Google+, hundreds of thousands of people joined.

- **Google owns the playing field.** Google can do more than merely tilt the playing field, because it *owns* the playing field. For example, Google integrated Google+ into search results, and Samsung phones and tablets come with the Google+ application pre-installed. Google bought Motorola's phone business, so we can assume similar integration will happen with Motorola phones and tablets too. Gmail account holders automatically have a Google+ account. In the future, Chrome, Google's browser which recently passed Firefox in popularity, will incorporate Google+ also.

When you add up these factors, Google brings indomitable power to Google+—roughly equal, I'd say, to Apple having Steve Jobs as a CEO. (This statement is a compliment to both Google and Steve.)

PERCEPTIONS, PEOPLE, PICTURES, OR PASSIONS?

The key to social media is to use the right tool for the job. Not "everyone" should use Facebook or Twitter or Pinterest or Google+, because everyone's needs are different. Moreover, these services are not mutually exclusive, so you can use each for different purposes. Still, the question remains: Should you use Google+? Here's how to decide:

Twitter = Perceptions. Twitter is great for getting or sending immediate perceptions such as witnessing news and events. In other words, if you want to learn that there was an earthquake in Chile before CNN and you like getting updates from Chileans at ground zero, then Twitter is for you. In short, Twitter is for real-time **perceptions.**

For Twitter, think Speakers' Corner, Hyde Park, London, where on Sunday afternoons, anyone can get up on a soapbox and speak about almost anything.

Facebook = People. Facebook is the way to learn what's going on in the lives of people you already know (friends, relatives, and colleagues). It's great for learning that their cats rolled over, that they went to a great party, or that they had sex, kittens, or children. In short, Facebook is for **people.**

For Facebook, think "Best Friends Forever."

Pinterest = Pictures. Pinterest is an online bulletin board where people post pictures of what they consider beautiful, cool, and neat. Where pictures are 5 percent of the action on Twitter and 25 percent of the action on Facebook and Google+, they are 95 percent of the action on Pinterest. Pinterest is light, playful, and fun. In short, Pinterest is for **pictures.**

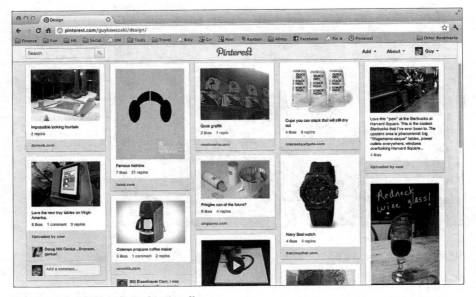

For Pinterest, think pictures of cool stuff.

Google+ = Passions. Google+ enables you to pursue your passions with people you don't know. Your 200 friends and family on Facebook may not share your passion for photography, but on Google+ you can have a blast with a community of photographers (I'll explain how shortly). In short, Google+ is for **passions.**

CONCLUSION

Do you want to enhance and expand the number of people who share your passions and interact with them via posts

For Google+ think: meeting people who share your passions (photo credit: Peter Adams).

and comments? If you do, focus on Google+. If you don't, stick with Facebook, Twitter, and LinkedIn until Google+ reaches critical mass. If you just want to have fun posting pictures of cool stuff, use Pinterest.

The Social Media Decoder by Dan Roam, founder of the Napkin Academy (www.napkinacademy.com) and author of *The Back of the Napkin*, *Unfolding the Napkin*, and *Blah Blah Blah*.

Or, you may decide you need multiple services: Twitter for perceptions, Facebook for people, Pinterest for pictures, and Google+ for passions. That's OK too.

How to Get Started

> *Vitality shows in not only the ability to persist but the ability to start over.*
>
> F. Scott Fitzgerald, "The Crack-Up"

Google+ Terminology

Here's a quick summary of social-networking terms so you can feel right at home on Google+. At some level, every service performs similar functions, so you'll feel right at home in a short time and sound like you've been using Google+ since the beta test started in June 2011.

Facebook	Twitter	Google+
Update or share (verb)	Tweet	Post or share
News feed (noun)	Timeline, stream, or feed	Stream
Timeline (noun)	Not applicable	Not applicable
Profile (noun)	Profile	Profile
Friend (verb)	Follow	Circle
Unfriend (verb)	Unfollow	Uncircle
Liked (verb)	Favorited	+1ed or plussed
Share (verb)	Retweet, RT, or via	Share or reshare
List (noun)	List	Circle
Friends (personal accounts) or fans (organizations and celebrities)	Followers	Followers

Facebook	Twitter	Google+
Video calling	Not applicable	Hangout
Not applicable	Verified account (noun)	Verified account
Common name (noun)	Handle	Common name
Tag with "+" or "@" (noun and verb)	Mention or @mention	+Mention with "+" or "@"
Message (noun and verb)	Direct message or DM	Private message
Not applicable	Hashtag (noun)	Hashtag
Fan page (noun)	Not applicable	Page
Not applicable	Follow Friday	Circle Sunday

SIGN UP

Since Google can divert the river and owns the playing field, you may find it hard to avoid Google+. In case you haven't run across it, you can sign up at http://accounts.google.com/SignUp for a Google account that enables you to use all the Google products. This takes less than a minute.

Keep your name simple—for example, using your first name and your last name. Do this right because it's hard to make a name change stick—this is akin to changing your company or product name after you've launched.

A simple name will make it easier for people to remember you and find your Google+ post. To wit, it's easier to remember and type in "Guy Kawasaki" than "G. Kawasaki," "GT Kawasaki," or "G. T. Kawasaki." There's a world of difference when people search for "Guy Kawasaki" versus "G Kawasaki."

Start Circling People

Signing up for a Google account.

Now you're at the party, but you don't know anyone yet, so the next step is to find people to "circle" ("friend" or "follow"). When you've circled approximately 50 people, Google+ gets really interesting. This process will only take a few minutes but will yield many hours of enlightenment, engagement, and enjoyment.

The first time you use Google+, you'll see a page like the one on page 14. (Note: Google is constantly updating the Google+ site, so what you see may differ from the pages and sequences that I show throughout this book. Don't sweat this—just poke around, and you'll be fine.)

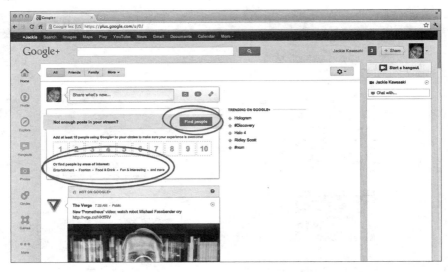

Initial screen after signing up.

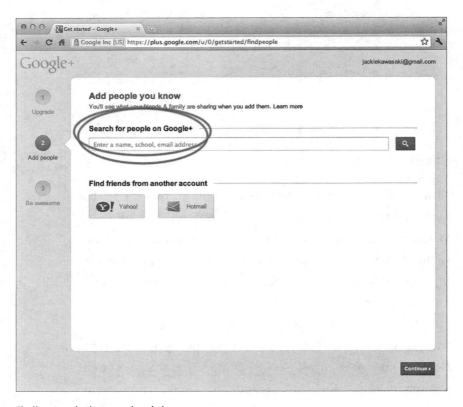

Finding people that you already know.

Google+ provides multiple options to get started. First, you can click on "Find people" to search for people you already know. Don't be disappointed if all your BFFs (best friends for life) aren't already on Google+—this is a chance to make new BFFs.

Second, you can click on categories of people such as "Entertainment," "Fashion," "Food & Drink," and "Fun & Interesting (see below)." Google compiled a list of "Picks" based on the fame and level of activity of the people. You can add these entire preselected circles or individual people. *

(There's an "*" at the end of the previous paragraph. I compiled a list of the best ways to evangelize Google+ in Chapter 15, "How to Evangelize Google+." I placed an "*" as a

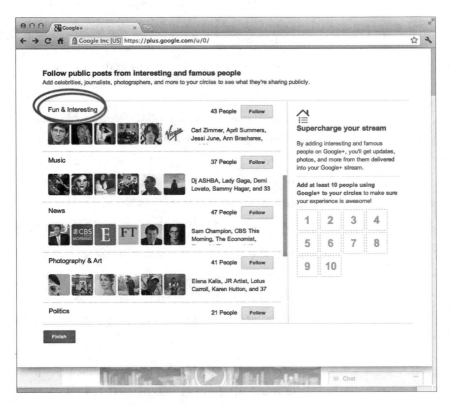

Finding "interesting and famous" people by clicking on the "Fun & Interesting" link.

marker throughout this book so that you can easily find these methods.)

However, fame and true interaction are usually inversely proportional, and if *People* has written about a person, his or her "people" may be doing the interacting. Here are a few simple ways to decide whether to circle someone:

- Does the person have a pleasant profile photo? The lack of a profile photo indicates that the person is clueless, a newbie, or a spammer. When there is a photo, you can infer a lot about the person by the profile photo he or she uses even though my profile photo reminds some people of *Silence of the Lambs*.

- What's in the person's photo area? The lack of a photo again indicates cluelessness, newness, or spamminess. On the other hand, beautiful and clever photos show an element of good taste and thoughtfulness.

- How many people have circled the person? Lots of followers doesn't necessarily mean the person is worth circling, but it's a pretty good data point. There might not be a good reason for someone to have thousands of followers, but there's usually a bad reason someone only has a handful of followers.

- When was the last time the person shared a post? This will show if the person is active on Google+. There's no sense following someone who is not active because the purpose of circling a person is to generate interaction.

- Are the person's posts +1ed, shared by many people, and commented upon? (I'll explain these terms soon.) People who share posts that generate more

than 10 shares and more than 10 comments tend to
be interesting.

An easy way to check out a person is to use Chrome,
Google's browser, and install a Chrome browser extension
called "CircleCount." Then when you mouse over a person's
name, you'll see the follower history and the average number of shares and comments. (You should try using Chrome
because it optimizes your Google+ experience and is a very
good browser in its own right.)

Checking out a person using CircleCount.

How to Navigate Google+

Now that you've circled a few people, it's time to explore how
to navigate Google+. You'll see a web page that looks like
the one on page 18. The top part of the window containing
white type on a black background is a way to navigate most of
Google's services such as Search, Maps, and Gmail. The nine
buttons in the vertical navigation ribbon on the left side are
the primary ways to navigate Google+ itself.

Navigating the Google+ page.

Here's what the buttons do:

- **Home.** Unlike the old saying, on Google+, home is where the "stream" is. This button displays your "stream" of what the people you follow have posted. You don't have to read every post any more than you have to read every story in your newspaper. Think of **Home** as your "news feed."

- **Profile.** When you want to see what you've posted, click on this button. It will show you all your posts, and it's a good way to manually check for new comments on your posts. Think of your **Profile** as your own blog or journal.

- **Explore.** If you'd like to find out "what's new and interesting" on Google+, this is the button for you. It will take you to a page that explains the cool features of Google+ as well as the posts that have the most comments and shares. Think of **Explore** as a way to find cool stuff.

- **Events.** You can use Events to plan and invite people to your parties, meetings, and Google+ hangouts. You create an invite, choose a theme picture, set a day and time, invite people and circles of people. You can think of **Events** as Evite for Google+.

- **Photos.** This button takes you to photo collections, including those you and your friends have posted as well as photos you've been tagged in. Think of **Photos** as a big photo album.

- **Circles.** You create circles in order to organize and filter who you interact with. Circling on Google+ does not involve sending people a "friend" request as on Facebook. You circle people unilaterally without their permission, although they are notified that you circled them. Think of **Circles** as a way of organizing collections of people.

- **Local.** Google Local helps you find "recommended places" such as restaurants and hotels near your geographic location. It provides Zagat scores and summaries plus the recommendations of people you know on Google+ and "top reviewers." Think of **Local** as your *Yellow Pages*.

- **Games.** Games is the front door to playing games on Google+. You have control over "when you see games, how you play them, and with whom you share your experiences." Think of **Games** as Dave & Busters.

- **Hangouts.** Hangouts is a killer feature of Google+ that enables you to have a video chat session with up to nine other people. You could, for example, get your family on a hangout and discuss that latest developments in quantum physics or the Stanley Cup playoffs. We'll discuss hangouts more in Chapter 9, "How to Hang out and How to Chat." Think of **Hangouts** as Skype on steroids.

- **More.** The More button enables you to add navigation buttons such as Pages and anything you've previously removed. **Pages** provides links to the pages that you have created or have access to. (Pages are Google+ accounts for organizations as opposed to people.) Think of **More** as a customization tool for your navigation ribbon.

By dragging and dropping these buttons, you can change their order. You can also drag a button off to the side, and it will disappear from the navigation ribbon. If you'd like to add back a button, click "More" to select it.*

More Google+ Assistance

There are more ways Google+ helps you find people to circle. After all, if Google can't help you find relevant search results, what can?

First, you can search for people at any time by using the Google+ search area (as opposed to the regular Google search area). When you find a person, Google+ also displays more people who might interest you (see the example on page 21). You can specify exact matches by adding quotation marks to your search in order to narrow results.

Second, you can enter keywords that describe your inter-ests and passions. For example, try words such as "knitting," "photography," "adoption," "UCLA," "UC Berkeley," "Macin-tosh," or "football." The results of a keyword search change significantly before and after clicking on the blue magnifying glass. Initially, Google+ takes its best shot at finding people. After the search, it displays people, posts, people, and pages.*

Searching for people you know.

A keyword search for "knitting" before clicking on the blue magnifying glass shows only people.

After clicking on the blue magnifying glass, Google+ provides posts
("Most recent" and "Best of"), people, and pages.

A word like "adoption" is used in many contexts such
as babies, pets, and new products, so the more "niche" the
term, the better. For example, "football" can refer to what
Americans call soccer as well as the high school, college, and
professional game with an oblong leather object. If you want
to find Green Bay Packers fans, a search for "Packers" would
work better than "football."

The result of your search can include "everything" which
means people, pages, posts, sparks (keyword searches of news),
and hangouts from your circles, from you, and from locations
(see page 23). Click on the "Everything" next to the search
term under the search entry area to make your choices.

When you find people who share your sensibilities, circle
them so you may continue to read their posts. Then take
the additional step of reading the comments on their posts.
Comments provide much of the magic of Google+, and they
can also help you find people to circle, too.

Third, as mentioned before, you can import your address book from other services, so that you can invite your friends and family to join you on Google+. This is a great way to add your existing relationships to Google+.

Fourth, you can add people to circles from your Gmail contacts database. Google+ is deeply integrated into Gmail, so you can even use circles to filter your e-mail.

Determining the breadth of your search results.

Use the Work of Others

Early adopters of Google+ realized that new members had difficulty finding people to circle, and they did something about it. (The fact that so many "evangelists" worked so hard on this problem is another similarity to the Macintosh phenomenon and bodes well for Google+.)

- **Compiled shared circles.** People have compiled thematic circles and shared them so that others may benefit from their research. Here are three: Chris

Porter's database of circles, Gabriel Vasile's list of popular circles, and the Public Circles Database.

(https://docs
.google.com
/spreadsheet/ccc
?key=0Ao1OX3UN
25EvdHRWR3lwW
XQ0a0RhWnFuW
ml5RnJHdkE&hl=
en_US#gid=0)

(https://plus
.google.com
/10639347869
5568433143
/posts/3CGaFR
VrGK8?hl=en)

(http://
publiccircles.
appspot.com/)

- **Shared-circle search.** You can search for every kind of shared circle by typing in "shared a circle with you" including the quotation marks in the Google+ search bar. (Hat-tip to Mike Elgan for this idea.) This will display all the circles that people have recently shared.

Searching for all shared circles.

To find a smaller number of shared circles, type in "shared a circle with you" (again, with the quotation marks) and then a keyword such as "Packers" to find shared circles about the Green Bay Packers football team (it doesn't matter if you include quotation marks around "Packers").

Once you've found a circle that you like, click on the blue "View shared circle" and then create a new circle for it or add the people to an existing circle.

Adding a circle.

Creating a new circle or adding to an existing circle from a shared circle.

You can select individuals from the shared circle by clicking on them—you do not need to add the entire circle.

- **Compilation sites.** Early adopters of Google+ compiled lists of people according to interest and expertise. As with the database of shared circles, you'll find hundreds of topics, so you're likely to find many people to follow.

  - Find People on Plus: http://findpeopleonplus.com

  - GGLPLS: www.gglpls.com

  - Google+ Counter: http://gpc.fm

  - GPEEP: www.gpeep.com

  - Group/AS: www.group.as

  - Plus Friend Finder: http://plusfriendfinder.com

  - Recommended Users: www.recommendedusers.com

  - Suggested Circles: http://suggestedcircles.com

- **Ranking sites.** Several sites rank people according to their number of followers and level of activity. The sites are useful for finding popular people, but don't assume that popular equals interesting, intelligent, or worth circling.

  - CircleCount: www.circlecount.com/populartotal

  - Social Statistics: http://socialstatistics.com/top/people/followers

CONCLUSION

There are a plethora of ways to find cool people who share your sensibilities and passions on Google+. You may not know these people or have even heard of them before, but they (and you) will make Google+ interesting. Spend a few minutes finding people, and you'll reap hours of enjoyment in return.

Additional Documentation on Google's Website
Note: At the end of each chapter, I will provide a link (or links) to additional information on Google's website.

Search

 (http://support.google.com/plus/bin/answer.py ?hl=en&answer=1669519&topic=1669512&ctx =topic)

How to Master Circles and Streams

> *You only have as many animals as the ecosystem can*
> *support and you only have as many friends as you*
> *can tolerate the bitching of.*
>
> RANDY K. MILHOLLAND,
> "Something Positive"

SOCIAL SEGMENTATION

During the process of finding interesting people, you can organize them into circles such as family, colleagues at work,
hockey team, and classmates. Then you can use circles in two
ways: first, to share posts with specific groups of people; second, to read posts from specific groups.

Here is a comparison of how Google+'s circles compare
to Facebook's and Twitter's lists:

Function	Google+	Facebook	Twitter
Organize who you share posts with	Yes	Yes	No
Organize whose posts you see	Yes	Yes but limited control	Yes
Shareable with others	Yes	No	Yes

Circles are a powerful Google+ feature that Facebook and Twitter do not match. Facebook's lists are handy but few people use them—perhaps because they were unavailable when Facebook started and because most people only have friends and family on Facebook, so it's less necessary to segment them. (The primary segmentation happens when kids don't "accept" their parents' friend requests!)

Twitter's lists are useful for filtering content from categories of people—for example, scientists. As with Google+ circles, you can also share Twitter lists with others. However, you cannot use a Twitter list to determine who receives your posts.

There are two ways to populate your Google+ circles: First, you can create circles such as "Family," "Friends," and "Colleagues" if the type of relationship you have with them determines what you want to share with them and receive from them. The "Family" circle, for example, would only contain relatives.

Second, you can create circles such as "Knitters" and "Macintosh" if your common passions, interests, or sensibilities determine what you want to share with them and receive from them. Then the "Knitters" circle could contain family, friends, or colleagues.

REMOVING PEOPLE FROM CIRCLES

Circles are flexible, so you can create circles based on either of the aforementioned principles (by relationship or by interest), and people can appear in more than one circle.

Later, you can delete circles or completely redo them. The people in the circles don't see the name of the circles you put them in—so you could, for example, create a circle called "Buttheads."

You can remove anyone from a circle by going to the circle and clicking on the "X" in the upper-right corner of the person's photo.

Note that circling is unilateral—that is, you don't have to ask for and receive permission to circle someone. Uncircling people is also much less emotional and personal than ending a "friendship" on Facebook, so tweak your circles without hesitation.

Also, uncircling people who are in your Gmail contacts database will not remove them from your contacts database. Similarly, if you delete someone from your contacts database, he or she will not be automatically uncircled.

Removing Scott Monty, head of social media for Ford, from one of my circles because he didn't send me a GT 500 Shelby Mustang for my birthday.

CIRCLES AND WHO SEES YOUR POSTS

Circles enable you to control who can read your posts. As I explained in the preface, I didn't understand at first that when you share a post with a specific circle, only people in that circle can read it. There are in fact four options for using circles to determine who can read your posts:

- **Public.** Anyone on the Internet can see your posts, and your posts also will appear in anyone's search results. I use this setting **99.9 percent of the time.**

- **Your circles.** Anyone who is in at least one of your circles will see your posts. You can control which circles are in "Your circles" by customizing your settings (at www.google.com/settings/plus).

- **Extended circles.** The people in your circles and the people in their circles can see your posts if you publicly display who you've circled on your profile.

- **Circles.** You can select the specific circle or circles that see your posts. This limits the exposure of these posts, although not in a bulletproof way, as I'll explain shortly.

Choosing who can see your posts.

RELEVANCY, NOT PRIVACY

Before you go nuts attempting to use circles as a privacy method, "lock" the posts that you don't want people to reshare with their followers. Otherwise, for example, a student could share a post with her school friends, and any of them could reshare that post with her parents.

Locking a post to prevent it from being reshared.

Of course, even if you lock the post, people can still copy and paste your text, take a screenshot of your photo, and share it with others. In other words, privacy is an illusion, and nothing is truly private once you press the "Share" button. Don't be paranoid, but don't be stupid, either.

A better way to think of circles is as a method to increase the relevancy of posts to groups of people rather than to ensure privacy. For example, a photo of my team that won a beer-league hockey championship might only be relevant to my hockey circle—if that.

Sharing Circles

You can share your circles with others. This is a fabulous way to help your followers find new people to circle. For example, if you compiled a circle of the best knitters on Google+, you can share this circle with your followers to help them find people who share a passion for knitting.

(https://plus
.google.com
/11070130
780396259
5019/posts
/RZpvrvXbeDT)

I found a bunch of science geeks to circle via this post by Fraser Cain. All I had to do was click on "Add circle" to start following several hundred people who share stories about science. When I, in turn, shared this circle with my followers, members of the circle told me that they gained hundreds of followers.

You can also add a circle for a short-term purpose. For example, Robert Scoble shared a circle of tech writers who were likely to cover the Consumer Electronics Show (CES) in January 2012. People could add this circle for the short duration of the show to get the latest news and then

(https://plus
.google.com
/111091089
5277274208
53/posts/boE
EJQKeL7U)

delete the circle afterward if they so desired. Even better, people could "silence" the circle (I'll explain how to do this shortly) after the show and then reactivate it during the next big tech event.

Circles and Your Stream

The flow of posts that you see is called your "stream." You access the stream by clicking on the "Home" button. The primary determinant of what's in your stream is the members of your circles.

You might become too successful at finding good stuff—or simply want to reduce the volume of your stream. You can adjust the quantity of posts you see from each circle by doing the following:

Click on the "Home" button.

Click on the name of a circle to the right of the "Home" button. If you don't see a circle's name, click on the "More" button.

Adjust the quantity of posts you'd like to see from that circle by using the slider.

For example, you can choose to see all posts from your family but fewer from your circle of tech friends and even fewer from your hockey circle. Or you can silence a circle completely. Why would you create a circle if you didn't want to read its posts? There are two reasons: first, to temporarily silence a circle but read its posts at another time, such as during the next tech show for the situation I described earlier; second, to share your posts with members of the circle but not read their posts.

In this case, I want to see most of the posts from my circle called "Friends."

Finally, you can click on a circle and make it the only visible stream. For example, if you want to read your family's posts and nothing else. Many people put me in a separate circle because I share so many posts. By doing so, they can choose to read my posts only at a convenient time. Unfortunately, the selection of a circle doesn't "stick," so you have to reselect the circle when you open a new browser window or change computers.

"What's Hot" and Hashtags

Google and the community have created two additional ways to increase the quality of your stream:

- **"What's hot."** Google compiles content that is "exemplary, interesting, and appropriate" to show you "serendipitous and diverse information." You get to it by clicking on "Explore" in the left sidebar.

Selecting "What's hot."

You'll see a collection of stories that Google decided would interest you. It provides a rich and eclectic selection of cool stuff, so give it a try sometime. And there's a slider bar to adjust volume that works in the same way as adjusting volume from a circle.

- **Hashtags.** A hashtag is the "#" symbol followed by a word. People informally agree on the word (usually called the "keyword") so that the community can find posts about a subject.

    For example, "#bacon" is in many posts about bacon. To get started with hashtags, search for "#" followed by the keywords that describe topics that interest you. You'll see that Google+ autocompletes hashtags to help you discover which tags to use.

    To find the posts that the bacon-loving community has shared with the specific inclusion of the hashtag "#bacon," search for "#bacon" and include the quotation marks—typing not simply *#bacon* but "*#bacon.*"

    You can then select the context in which the hashtag is used, including everything, people and pages, posts, and more.

    This is a list of interesting and eclectic hashtags. You'll see two that include the names of days of the week: #ScienceSunday and #BuggyFriday. This refers to the day of the week when people use the hashtag.

- #Bacon (https://plus.google.com/s/"bacon")

- #BuggyFriday (https://plus.google.com /s/"buggyfriday")

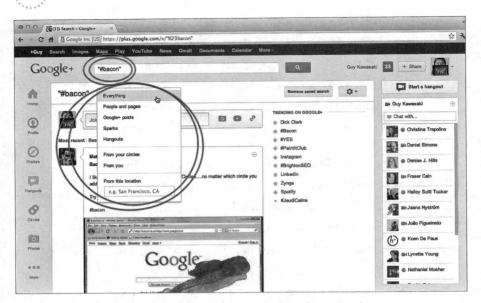

Include the quotation marks to find posts containing a hashtag then select the contexts in which people used the hashtag.

- #Food (https://plus.google.com/s/"food")

- #Gadgets (https://plus.google.com/s /"gadgets")

- #Photography (https://plus.google.com/s /"photography")

- #ScienceSunday (https://plus.google.com/s /"sciencesunday")

- #Social Media (https://plus.google.com/s /"socialmedia")

When you create a hashtag search (or any other search) that you like, click on "Save this search," and it will be saved in the left sidebar for you to access in the future.

Conclusion

Circles are one of the most important Google+ concepts because they enable you to segment your relationships on the
service. This means you can fine-tune the stream of content
that you consume as well as determine what content people
receive from you. Tweaking your circles is a good investment
to optimize your Google+ experience.

Additional Documentation on Google's Website

Circles

 (http://support.google.com/plus/bin/answer.py
?hl=en&answer=1047805&topic=1257347&ctx
=topic)

Google+ Safety Center

 (http://www.google.com/+/safety/)

Streams

 (http://support.google.com/plus/bin/topic.py?hl
=en&topic=1257360&parent=1257347&ctx
=topic)

How to Make an Enchanting Profile

> *When I'm working on a problem, I never think*
> *about beauty. I think only how to solve the problem.*
> *But when I have finished, if the solution is not*
> *beautiful, I know it is wrong.*
>
> R. BUCKMINSTER FULLER

An enchanting profile is crucial because people look at profiles and make snap judgments about whether you're worth paying attention to and worth circling. This chapter explains how to edit and optimize them.

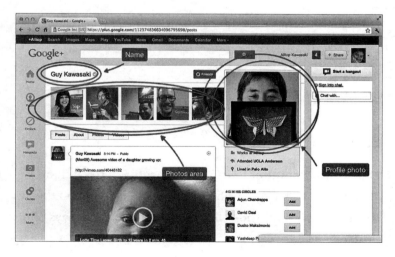

What people
see when
they click on
"Posts."

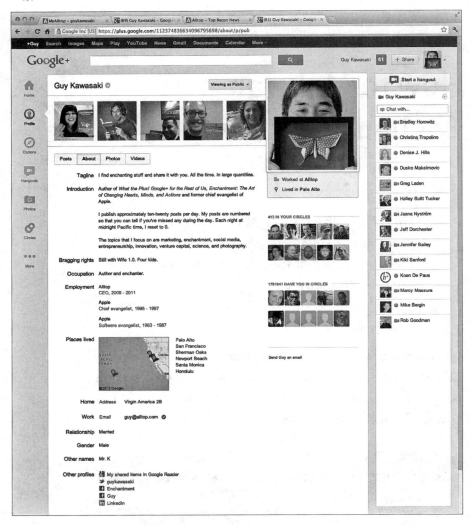

What people see when they click on "About."

Editing Your Profile

The starting point of editing your profile is to click on the "Profile" button in the Google+ navigation ribbon on the left side of the window. Then click on the blue box that says "Edit profile."

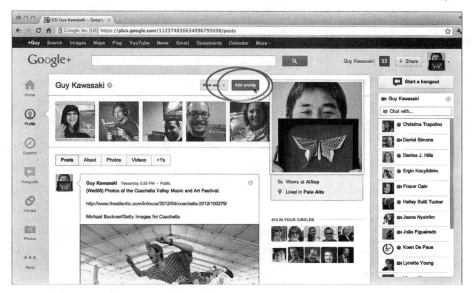

Getting to the profile editing page.

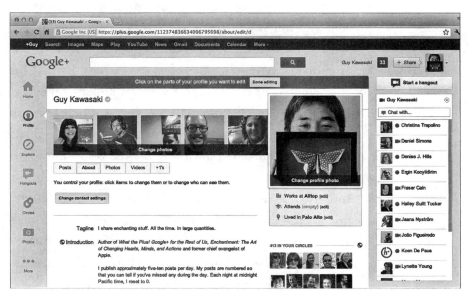

The profile editing page.

Now you can edit your profile page. There are five areas: name, photos, profile photo, contact settings, and biographical information.

NAME

The initial registration process created your Google+ name. If you haven't registered yet, let me remind you to keep your name as simple as possible so that people can easily find you and your posts.

You can also use a nickname in addition to your regular name. To add a nickname, go to your profile, click on "Edit Profile," select your name, click on "More options," and add your nickname. If Google suspects your nickname isn't legitimate, you'll have to provide references to your use of it in the news, a copy of your driver's license, or proof of a large following on another social-media service.

Your Google+ account will have a friendly format such as http://plus.google.com/112374836634096795698 which is not exactly a vanity URL like http://www.facebook.com/guy. However, you can use a service called gplus.to (http://gplus .to) or gplusid (www.gplusid.com) to create a vanity URL for Google+. You'll need the 21-digit account number—for example, "112374836634096795698" is my account number. You can grab it from the URL when you're on your profile or posts page. Then send the custom URL to people who want to locate you on Google+.

You may notice a check mark ($\sqrt{}$) within a gray circle next to some people's names. This signifies that Google+ has verified their identity. Verification is done to ensure that the accounts of celebrities, egomaniacs, and narcissists are the real thing. You need to contact Google to ask it to verify your account in you're a celebrity, egomaniac, or narcissist.

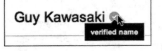

The √ means it's a verified account.

The reason to keep your name simple is the "+mentions" in posts and comments. When you type in the + sign and then a person's name, Google+ will display the names that match so that you can select the right individual. First Google+ presents the people in your circles and then it searches outside your circles.

Creating a +mention.

The people who you've +mentioned will receive an e-mail notification (unless they turned off notifications) that you mentioned them. This is a useful capability that increases the likelihood that people see your comments, responses, and mentions of them—especially people with lots of mentions.*

+Mentions enhance the Google+ experience by making it more interactive. The ability to receive +mention notifications is one of my favorite features of Google+ because I like to respond to people. However, don't set yourself up for disappointment by +mentioning famous people just to see if you can get them to read your posts and respond to you. That's not a proper use of +mentions.

PHOTOS

The photos area is beneath your name. It can display from one to five photos or GIFs. If a picture is worth a thousand words, Google+ is giving you 5,000 words to express yourself.

Click on the photos area to edit it. Then you can pick landscape, "cover photo" template or the five-photo template. The dimensions of the cover photo are 940 × 180 pixels. The dimensions of the five-photo template are 110 × 110 pixels. Click on "Add Photo" in order to upload photos for the photos area.

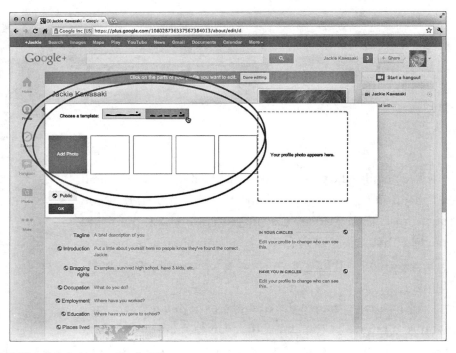

Editing the photos area the first time.

The first five photos in the album are the ones that appear in the photos area. You don't have to use five photos, but your page may look strange without five. You can change these five photos and reorder them later.

Editing the photos area after you've already placed photos in your album.

The photos area is the best place to communicate what's important to you and where you can get whimsical and personal. My photos area contains five photos of people holding *Enchantment* in order to communicate that lots of people are reading my book. I change the photos every two weeks or so.

My photos area.

If you want to show your cat, dog, baby, car, or logo, this is the place to do it—not in your profile photo. Here are other examples of good photo areas:

Dave Powell's scrapbook shows that he likes Japan and Audis.

Allison Sekuler's scrapbook shows that she loves science.

Mari Smith's scrapbook shows that she published a book, is my buddy, spoke at Google, visited Facebook, and is much taller than Suze Orman.

Finally, if you'd like to impress your followers with your graphics ability, you can use one picture and split it into five pieces using Gpluspic (http://gpluspic.com).

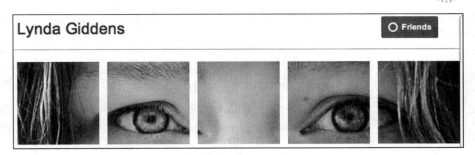

The photos area of Lynda Giddens is a good example of a photo split into five pieces.

Do not, unless you want to look clueless, leave your photos area empty, so that it looks like this to people.

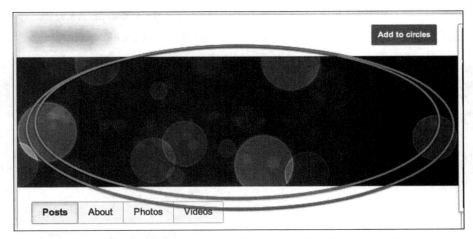

What happens if you leave your photos area blank.

PROFILE PHOTO

Your profile photo is usually the first thing people see about you, and people being people, they'll make an instant judgment. You may think these tips about profile photo are "duh-isms," but I see crappy profile photos every day. The dimensions of the profile photo are 250 × 250 pixels. Here's how to create an enchanting profile photo:

- **Show your face.** Don't use a logo, graphic, or cartoon. Find or take a photo where you have a "Duchenne smile" (the kind of smile that uses both the jaw and eye muscles, named after French neurologist Guillaume-Benjamin Duchenne). The goal is to look likable and trustworthy.

- **Use a tight shot.** Emphasize your face. It's not necessary nor desirable to show everyone in your family including your dog and the setting sun. You have 62,500 pixels at your disposal. Use them wisely.

- **Go asymmetrical.** Symmetry is overrated. Don't stick your face exactly in the middle of the photo. It's a lot more interesting off to one side or another. Professional photographers seldom place a face in the middle of a photo.

- **Do it well.** Ensure that your photo is in focus, your face is well lit, and there isn't any redeye. Don't use a cheesy photo from your 10-year-old, one-megapixel camera phone. You don't have to be Yousuf Karsh or Annie Leibovitz, but don't be a clown, either.

I stumbled upon a photo album by Kris Krüg of several hundred photos of people. He didn't create this album for this purpose, but it provides examples of photos that would make good profile photos. Also, here are examples of good profile photos from two of my friends on Google+:

Marcy Massura's profile photo shows that her head is in the clouds and that she's an Instagram fan.

This profile photo shows that
Peg Fitzpatrick is cheerful, charismatic,
and marvels at life.

CONTACT SETTINGS

Click on "Change contact settings" to control who can send
you a message or e-mail via your profile. I make it easy for
people to do this—my logic is you never know what opportunity might appear if you're accessible.

Changing
contact
settings.

BIOGRAPHICAL INFORMATION

The Profile page on Google+ outshines similar functionality on Facebook. Twitter, and Pinterest. Twitter, for example,

provides you with only 160 characters of space. This background section is a way to establish your coolness, credibility, and character.

- **Tagline.** This is your personal elevator pitch. Imagine you get in an elevator that's going from the second floor to the lobby. In the elevator is the hottest guy or gal you've ever seen, and out of the blue, he or she asks, "What do you do?"

  What will you say? "I live with my mother, and we have dead cats in our refrigerator." "I am the master of disaster." "I deliver mail at Goldman Sachs." I don't think so. Or, at least I hope not.

- **Introduction.** This time, imagine that you get in an elevator that's going from the fifth floor to the lobby, so you've got much more time to talk. In the elevator is the hottest guy or gal you've ever seen. He or she asks you who you are. That's what the introduction is for.

- **Bragging rights.** My theory is that Google included this field as a test to see who is clueless. Pass the test by restraining and underselling yourself or bragging about something sensible such as being happily married as opposed to driving a car made by a company whose name ends in "i" (other than Audi).

- **Occupation.** Keep it short, serious, and accurate, yet enticing. You are the only person who thinks "master of disaster" is clever. Everyone else thinks it's dorky.

- **Employment.** Imagine that you are applying for your dream job, and that the company will check your work history. This is a way to establish credibility ("you worked at Apple!") and professional connections.

When people mouse-over your name, they'll see what's either in the occupation or employment field. I've seen both fields used, and I don't know how Google+ decides which one to display.

- **Education.** Again, you're applying for your dream job, and the company will verify your educational background. This is also a way to establish credibility and make connections with fellow alumni.

- **Places lived.** This is an opportunity to demonstrate your worldliness and establish connections with people with similar pasts or roots.

- **Home.** You don't have to put in your precise address or display this field. The city and state/country is enough. Many people want to socialize with people who live and work close by.

- **Work.** Treat this the same way as your home address.

- **Relationship.** This is your call—to either attract people or dissuade them.

- **Looking for.** This is another opportunity to make a fool of yourself, so show some restraint.

- **Gender.** Surely you don't need my advice for this.

- **Other names.** You can enter your maiden name, alternate spellings, and other names that people might know you by.

- **Profile discovery.** This is where you determine whether people can find your profile via a Google+ search. By definition, if you're on Google+ you probably want to be found, so I would enable discovery.

- **Other profiles.** Add your other social-media accounts on Facebook, Twitter, LinkedIn, and additional networks for people who want to learn more about you. Ensure that your other profiles are consistent or only include the ones that are consistent with how you position yourself on Google+.

- **Contributor to.** If you have a blog or contribute to other websites, this is the place to provide this information.

- **Recommended links.** This section is akin to your scrapbook. You can show the breadth, depth, and whimsy of your soul here.

After editing your profile, click on the button that says "Done editing" and then click on "View as . . ." to see your profile as others do.

Seeing your profile as others see it.

MOUSING OVER

When people mouse over your name, they will see your photos area, your profile photo, and limited biographical information such as your current company. This info is grabbed from your profile.

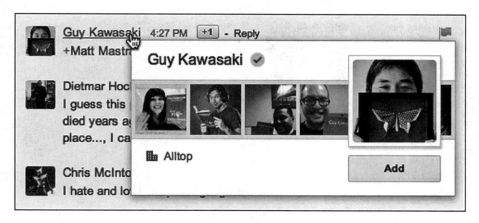

What people see when they mouse over a name.

CONCLUSION

Your Google+ profile is your résumé, a sales pitch, and a window into your soul. Many people don't even add a profile photo or fill out the information. It's one of the primary ways that people will judge you on Google+, so spend an hour or two to make it enchanting.

Additional Documentation on Google's Website

Google+ Privacy Policy

 (http://www.google.com/intl/en/policies/)

Names

(http://support.google.com/plus/bin/answer
.py?hl=en&answer=1228271)

Profiles

(http://support.google.com/plus/bin/answer.py
?hl=en&answer=1057172&topic=1257354&ctx
=topic)

CHAPTER

4+

How to Achieve Trustworthiness

> *We should give as we would receive, cheerfully,*
> *quickly, and without hesitation; for there is no grace*
> *in a benefit that sticks to the fingers.*
>
> SENECA, *Morals*

A SHORT COURSE IN TRUSTWORTHINESS

An enchanting profile is necessary, but not sufficient, to successfully using Google+. To take your presence to the next level, you need to project trustworthiness. Take it from the guy who wrote the book on *Enchantment*; here are the best ways for doing so:

- **Show up.** You get points on Google+, just as in life, for showing up—that is, for sharing, commenting, and adding to the flow of information. You don't need to pen Pulitzer Prize–quality stuff—sharing posts two to three times a day and commenting on three to five posts of other people for a few months allows people to get to know you. Familiarity breeds consent.

- **Make the community better.** People trust folks who add value to the Google+ community. People distrust people who don't. It's that simple, so try to help someone every day. This can take many forms: technical assistance, pointing to online resources, and even simple empathy for the plight of others. Give without expectation of return, and ironically, you'll probably increase the returns that you reap.

- **Don't be an orifice.** If you want a trustworthy reputation, don't attack folks or denigrate their efforts. Stay positive. Stay uplifting. Or stay silent. Let someone else be the orifice—there are plenty of volunteers. Like my mother used to say, "If you don't have anything good to say, shut up."

- **Keep it clean.** There's a high correlation between being an orifice and frequent swearing. My advice is that you should hardly ever swear—once or twice a year for the rare time that you need to make a profound impact. Frequent profanity is the enemy of trustworthiness.

- **Trust others first.** If you want to be trusted, you have to trust others first. This isn't a chicken-and-egg issue—there's a definite sequence: you trust, then you're trusted. Give people the benefit of the doubt and assume that they are good until proven bad. For example, I trusted 240 strangers with the manuscript for this book.

- **Disclose your interests.** There's nothing wrong with making a living and using Google+ to do so. What's wrong is if you don't disclose conflicts of interest or if you are promoting things more than 5 percent of the time. For example, when I shared three posts about Microsoft Office templates for raising money, I added the text "Promotional consideration paid by Microsoft." I took some heat for doing a promotion, but not for trying to hide it.

- **Gain knowledge and competence.** People trust experts, so discuss what you really know or become an expert and a reliable resource. Or, make people aware of what you know if you're already an expert. Don't jeopardize your credibility by expressing yourself about topics that are outside your expertise.

- **Bake a bigger pie.** There are two kinds of people: eaters and bakers. Eaters think the world is a zero-sum game: what you eat, someone else cannot eat, so they eat as much as they can. Bakers think that the world is not a zero-sum game—they can just bake more and bigger pies. Everyone can eat more. People trust bakers and not eaters.

- **Resist bad means.** The use of bad means to achieve good ends is a slippery slope that has caused the downfall of many people throughout history, not just in this era of social media. When you find yourself justifying actions—for example spamming people— for a good cause, double-check what you're doing.

CONCLUSION

Don't get the impression that the key to trustworthiness is simply *projecting* trustworthiness. That would be putting lipstick on a pig—it's still a pig underneath. The underlying fundamentals are the key, so that you can be *conveying* trustworthiness.

If you are a good and honest person at your core and you project it, you'll enjoy a trustworthy reputation on Google+ and such a reputation will make your Google+ experience all the better.

CHAPTER 5

How to Comment

> *The skill of writing is to create a context in which other people can think.*
>
> EDWIN SCHLOSSBERG

BREAKING THE SILENCE

Now that you've found interesting people to follow, created an enchanting profile, and honed your trustworthiness, the next step is to make a dent in the Google+ universe by posting comments. This will enable you to:

- Provide positive feedback to the author of a post.

- Help the author and readers of posts.

- Express a difference of opinion with the author and other commenters.

- Interact with influencers, authorities, and leaders who probably wouldn't answer your e-mail if you wrote them one.

- Increase the value of the post with additional information and insights.

- Position yourself as an interesting and credible person worth circling.

- Find new people to circle.

You'd be surprised at the number of people who comment on posts solely in order to draw attention to themselves, attack others, and spam links to sites that no one in their right mind would visit. But you know better and won't do that.

Drive-By Comments

Before we get to long-form comments, there are several quick ways to provide feedback on posts. These "drive-by" comments require less effort and may be enough for what you want to communicate.

- **+1 = "Thanks for getting my car.** Here's a buck." A +1 is like a tip for the valet or bellman. Any single +1 is not a big deal, but as with tips, +1s can add up to significant compensation, so you should throw them around liberally. A +1 is the equivalent of a Facebook "like" and should be given and judged in the same way.

- **Share = "You've got to see this!"** You can "share" another person's post. This means that you like it so much that you're willing to bet your reputation by providing it to others. Finding something worth sharing is good, but adding value by appending new information is even better. If I had a choice between a comment and a share on my posts, I would pick the share because it increases the exposure of the post whereas a comment does not.

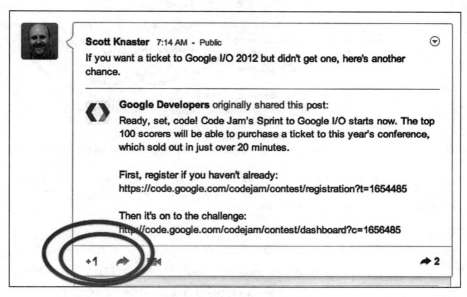

Scott Knaster 7:14 AM · Public
If you want a ticket to Google I/O 2012 but didn't get one, here's another chance.

Google Developers originally shared this post:
Ready, set, code! Code Jam's Sprint to Google I/O starts now. The top 100 scorers will be able to purchase a ticket to this year's conference, which sold out in just over 20 minutes.

First, register if you haven't already:
https://code.google.com/codejam/contest/registration?t=1654485

Then it's on to the challenge:
http://code.google.com/codejam/contest/dashboard?c=1656485

+1

+2

+1 and sharing a post.

- **Share by e-mailing link = "You're such a late adopter that I'm sending you this the old-school way."** There's one more way to spread a Google+ post: copying the link for the post and forwarding it via e-mail or posting the link on other social-media services. There are two ways to copy the link. First, click on the time stamp of the post. Second, click on "Link to this post" in the drop-down arrow in the upper-right corner of the post. Note: the second method only works on public posts. Private or limited-share posts require clicking on the time stamp.

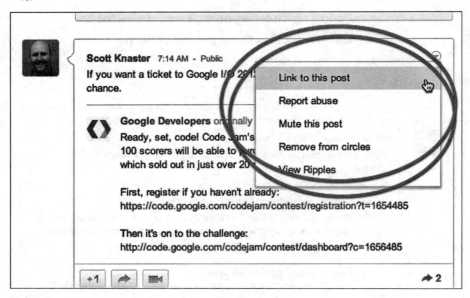

Clicking on "Link to this post" to obtain the post's URL.

- **One-word comments.** Many people make one-word comments such as "cool," "wow," "LOL," or "hah!" They do it to "join the party" out of sheer enthusiasm for the post. (When I see an NHL player score with a slap shot from 60 feet, all I can say is "Wow!" too.) So one-word comments are OK, but you've got a lot of space, so why not let it rip and show more emotion? "Cool, it rocks that you posted this," "Wow, this is totally cool," or "Please keep this kind of post coming, baby!" If you don't have the time or inclination to make a substantive comment, consider using a +1 instead.

+1s, shares, shares via e-mail, and one-word comments are not mutually exclusive, so you can do any combination of the three. In a perfect world, people would share the post with their followers, +1 it, *and* write a comment.

LONG-FORM COMMENTS: "THIS IS WHAT I THINK"

The quality, breadth, and depth of Google+ comments compared to Facebook, Twitter, and Pinterest blow me away. This level of interaction separates Google+ from those other services, and it's the reason Robert Scoble and thousands of other early adopters love Google+.

A good model for long-form comments is that you are talking to people who have invited you into their homes for dinner. As a guest, you should show a high level of civility and class and behave in the following ways:

- **Create value.** Good comments make a post even better. This doesn't mean that people should only say positive things—negative feedback that is honest, supportive, and respectful is as valuable as positive feedback.

- **Stay on topic.** You can provide supplemental information and even add color and drama, but you must stay on topic. If I share a post about hockey, God bless you if you want to talk about other sports or even about your nonsports passions. But don't make a comment about why Newt Gingrich should be president. Certainly a link to your website is in poor form.

- **Show some class.** Refrain from profanity and the big three "isms": racism, sexism, and ageism. The fact that the world doesn't know you don't have class doesn't mean you should remove all doubt. Remember: you're a guest in someone's home.

- **Limit arguments to three rounds.** The best (and worst) interactions often occur between commenters. It's enchanting to watch strangers develop relationships and take posts in deeper and serendipitous (albeit related) directions. That's the good news. The bad news is that commenters sometimes get into knock-down fights and post mean-spirited comments that they would never utter in person.

   My suggestion is to embrace the rules of amateur boxing and fight for only three rounds. The opening bell is when the author shares a post. Round 1: Person A posts a comment. Round 2: Person B responds to the comment. Round 3: Person A responds to the response. End of fight—even if Person B responds again. If Person A and B want to go more rounds, they can start their own thread and fight someplace else.

- **"Reply to" the author with +mention.** Remember to type in "+" and then start typing the author's name until you see it pop up in a list of people with similar names. Then select the correct name, and it will turn blue and link to the author's profile.

- **"Reply" to another commenter.** You'll often reply to people who posted comments in a post shared by someone else. In this case, you should +mention the commenter and not the originator of the post. Ensure that you're +mentioning the right person.

THE ALL-IMPORTANT +MENTION

The +mention is so important that I'm dedicating a separate section to it. In the screenshot below, I got a Gmail notification of Michael Interbartolo's response. I did not get one for Dan Boissy's. On Facebook, similar functionality is called "@name," and on Twitter it's called an "@mention."

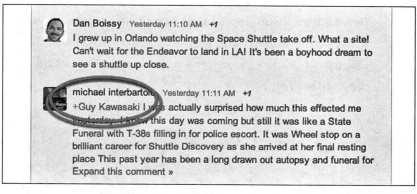

A +mention of me in comments means I'll get a notified via Gmail.

If you don't do a +mention, then it's less likely that the person you mentioned or replied to will know about your action. You are depending on the person manually checking old posts for new comments instead of getting notifications.

There are two ways to do a +mention. I explained how earlier, but in case you missed it, you type in a "+" and then start typing the person's name until it shows up in the list.

An easier way to create a +mention is to install a Chrome browser extension called "Replies and More for Google+." This extension makes it possible to "reply" to the author and commenters by adding a link to click on.

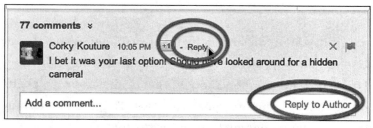

Using Replies and More for Google+ to reply to the commenter (Corky Kouture) or the author of the post.

Replies and More does one more cool thing: it enables you to share Google+ posts (yours or others) on Facebook and Twitter. It's the most valuable Google+ extension in the world, and I am amazed that Google hasn't added this functionality into Google+ so that installing an extension isn't necessary. Go ahead and install it now. (Note: when Google changes, Google+ extensions often cease to function until they are revised.)

Sharing a post on Twitter and Facebook with Replies and More.

And while you are at it, install Google Translate for Google+ so that you can read any comments you get in other languages. Remember, though, that Translate is a website taking its best shot at translating text. This is not the same thing as a fluent person translating the text.

Conclusion

The quality and quantity of comments on Google+ is one of the crown jewels of the service. By observing some simple practices, such as behaving like a guest and acting in a positive and constructive manner, you'll be a great commenter who makes Google+ even better.

Additional Documentation on Google's Website

+1

 (http://support.google.com/plus/bin/answer .py?hl=en&answer=1047397)

+1 Spelling Conventions

 (http://support.google.com/plus/bin/answer .py?hl=en&answer=1237207&topic=1207011&c tx=topic)

How to Share Posts

> *A scrupulous writer, in every sentence that he writes, will ask himself at least four questions, thus: 1. What am I trying to say? 2. What words will express it? 3. What image or idiom will make it clearer? 4. Is this image fresh enough to have an effect?*
>
> GEORGE ORWELL,
> *Politics and the English Language*, 1946

JUST HAVE FUN

The goodness of Google+ increases by an order of magnitude when you craft and share your own posts. Although many experts recommend strategizing about your goals for using a social medium, I advise you to loosely consider these conceptual questions:

- **Why are you using Google+?** Is your goal to brand yourself, meet new people, learn about social media, or generate business leads?

- **How do you want to position yourself on Google+?** For example, it could be as a content expert in entrepreneurship, a good dad, or an all-around nice guy.

- **What's your best guess for what interests your followers?** If you're a professional photographer, your followers may only want photographs and photography tips.

The answers to these questions determine your content, writing style, and frequency of posts. Generally, your posts to the public should be consistent with why you're using Google+, how you want to position yourself, and what people are looking to read by following you. Then you can use other, smaller circles for posts that are outside these boundaries—this is why circles are so important.

For example, if you're trying to establish yourself as an expert in venture capital and entrepreneurship, then most of your public posts should cover these topics. Then use your hockey and photography circles for your other passions in order to avoid dilution. (By the way, if you want to see the top photos on Google+ every day, check out PhotoExtract.com.)

On the other hand, don't overthink sharing. Eclecticism is a good thing, so after you establish a reputation for a particular expertise, then you can and should include posts about your other passions. This will make you more enchanting because you're multidimensional and "human." In any case, people will adjust and self-select whether they circle you.

You may even attract more followers if they see that your Google+ presence is richer and deeper than a single dimension. Also, if Google+ becomes a chore because you have to stick to a script, you won't enjoy it as much. At all times, remember what I like to call the first amendment of Google+: you have the right to post anything that you want.

Congress shall make no law respecting an establishment of religion, or prohibiting the free exercise thereof; or abridging the freedom

of speech, or of the press; or the right of the
people peaceably to assemble, and to petition
the Government for a redress of grievances.

FIRST AMENDMENT, US Constitution

BE A CURATOR

I salute anyone who can regularly generate content that's informative, analytical, helpful, amusing, or amazing. This is called "blogging." I did it for a few years, but I couldn't sustain blogging because I have a wife, four kids, one dog, two chickens, two turtles, three guinea pigs, and two lizards.

By necessity I became a curator, which means that I find good stuff and point people to it. Curating is a valuable skill because there is an abundance of good content but many people don't have the time to find it. The best curators find things before anyone else does. For example, Fraser Cain, the science-circle guy, monitors astrophotography forums to find new astrophotos and then shares them with his followers.

WHERE TO LOOK

How hard is it to find interesting stuff all the time? On a scale of 1 to 10, it's an 8 because curating takes knowing where to look and what to look for. How does one do this? Allow me to use a hockey analogy: a "face-off" is when the official drops the puck between two players, and they battle to control it. I asked Jamie Baker, a former San Jose Sharks player, how to win face-offs, and his response was, "Cheat." In other words, do whatever it takes.

Curating requires doing whatever it takes too. In other words, piggybacking on people and sites that are already curating content. I share posts five to ten times a day on Google+, and here are my main sources:

- **People you follow.** Cherry-pick what the people who you've circled have posted. (You followed them because they were interesting, right?) When you find an interesting post, click on "Share," add your own thoughts, and let it rip.

Step one
of sharing
someone
else's post.

Step two
of sharing
someone
else's post.

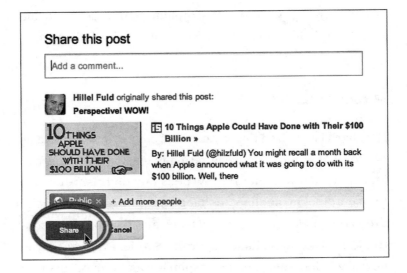

- **StumbleUpon.** StumbleUpon is a community of approximately 20 million people. They "stumble upon" websites and rate them. This enters the pages

into the StumbleUpon system for the rest of the
community. StumbleUpon has categorized websites
so that members can select topics such as gadgets,
design, or sports.

- **SmartBrief.** SmartBrief curates content for trade
associations. It employs people who pour over blogs
and websites in order to select the best articles.
You can benefit from this work because SmartBrief
makes its selections available to the public. For
example, to find stories about social media, use the
social-media SmartBrief page.

- **Pinterest.** Pinterest is a "virtual pinboard" that
people use to share "all the beautiful things you
find on the web." It's a great place to find cool stuff
to share with your followers. If appealing to female
(and increasingly male) followers is important to
you, Pinterest is a great source for content.

- **Alltop.** I am the cofounder of Alltop. Our goal is to
provide an online "magazine rack" of topics ranging
from A (Adoption) to Z (Zoology). Our researchers
selected RSS feeds from more than 25,000 websites
and blogs that cover more than 1,000 topics. Alltop
displays the headline and first paragraph of the
five most recent stories from each source. Let's
say you want to find stories about Google+, food,
photography, Macintosh, or adoption. Alltop will
take care of you.

- **HolyKaw.** I'm also the cofounder of HolyKaw (www
.HolyKaw.com). The purpose of this site is to find
20 to 30 stories every day that make you say, "Holy
cow!" (Holycow.com was taken, but since Kawasaki

is pronounced like "cow-asaki," I thought HolyKaw would work.) HolyKaw represents 20 intelligent people who are looking for good stuff.

- **The Big Picture and In Focus.** These sites represent Alan Taylor's vision of how to create photo essays about current events. He started with The Big Picture (http://www.boston.com/bigpicture/) as a feature on the *Boston Globe*'s website Boston.com and then moved to In Focus (http://www.theatlantic.com /infocus/) at *The Atlantic*. The photos on both sites are always breathtaking.

- **NPR.** NPR delivers great content every day of the year—remarkably so. My favorite shows are *TechNation, Fresh Air,* and *Wait, Wait Don't Tell Me.* You can find something every day on NPR that's worth posting.

- **TED.** TED produces some of the most intellectually stimulating videos in the world. Its 18-minute limit forces speakers to get to the point. The expansion of TED to local conferences makes this source even richer.

- **Futurity.** The basis of many stories in the mainstream news is press releases from research universities. Futurity enables you to beat the press because it publishes research findings from a consortium of universities in the United States, Canada, the United Kingdom, and Australia. An easy way to access Futurity is to use Futurity.alltop.com.

- **Specialized search engines.** The folks at OnlineUniversities.com compiled a list of 100 search engines. It includes links to sources such as the Library of Congress, NASA Historical Archive, and David Rumsey Map Collection. If you want to out-hardcore even the hardcore, this is the place for you.

What to Look For

Knowing where to look is half the battle. Knowing what to look for is the other half. There are five main categories of material to use as Google+ posts:

- **Information.** "What just happened?" Examples: Google incorporates Google+ circles into Gmail and new evidence on whether videogames are good or bad for kids.

 (http://www.futurity.org/society-culture /are-videogames-good-or-bad-%E2%80%A6 -or-both/#more-45891)

- **Analysis.** "What does it mean that this happened?" Example: Brian Solis explains the effect of a Twitter facelift.

 (http://www.briansolis.com/2011/12 /newnewtwitter/)

- **Assistance.** "How do I get this to happen for me?" (If it's a good thing.) Or, "How do I avoid this?" (If it's a bad thing.) Examples: how to get more Facebook comments and how to get your résumé past automated-screening software.

(http://fanpageflow.com/10-ideas-comments -facebook-posts/)

(https://plus.google.com/1123748366340967 95698/posts/44eTKKons4o)

- **Amusement.** "How funny is this?" Examples: a Diet Coke and Mentos–powered car or my family is going to raise chickens.

(http://www.youtube.com/watch?v =DhFwiFHWat8)

(https://plus.google.com/1123748366340967 95698/posts/7ZuccMRTNbp)

- **Amazement.** Can you believe this? Examples: jumping through a cave in a wingsuit with your mother watching or watching Canadians do a little skating.

(http://vimeo.com/33462353)

(http://www.youtube.com/watch?v=84i7
Yheey3g)

Extra Credit

In addition to information, analysis, assistance, amusement, and amazement, there are other types of posts that work well for me. (I can get away with more than most people, but I'm also held to a higher standard.) Here are some types of posts that I encourage you to try.

- **Studies.** People enjoy reading analyses of studies because it helps them stay on the cutting edge of research. Studies about social media, marketing, and security are popular on Google+.

- **Assistance.** I mentioned earlier that posts that *provide* assistance is effective, but you can also *request* assistance when you need help. For example, when I wrote this section of the book, I asked people about using some features of Google+ posting.

 (https://plus.google.com/1123748366340
96795698/posts/8PyYE4FhbUi)

- **Food and recipes.** People love food and recipes. You don't need to be a chef to pull this off. In fact, the less connected you are to stuffy haute cuisine, the better.

- **Everyday frustration.** Document an everyday frustration such as setting up a HP printer, the line for a taxi at the Las Vegas airport, or traffic in São Paolo and watch the empathetic comments roll in.

 (https://plus.google.com/112374836634096795698/posts/CiAzrns9QVV)

- **Everyday satisfaction.** Good experiences work too. For example, share how well wireless works on Virgin America, the access speed of Verizon 4G LTE, or how a genius at the Palo Alto Apple Store fixed your MacBook—after the store was closed!

 (https://plus.google.com/112374836634096795698/posts/HrjX1tmGXn9)

- **Titillation.** Titillation occurs when something cool happens to you. For example, Porsche loaned me a Panamera to drive for a week. People loved this post because they could live vicariously through my blind, dumb luck.

 (https://plus.google.com/photos/112374836634096795698/albums/5641333761588444593)

- **Celebs.** People love to discuss celebrities, so posts about famous folks generate comments—pro and con. Here's one about Wine Library TV founder

and tech celebrity Gary Vaynerchuk speaking in
Istanbul.

 (https://plus.google.com/11237483663409
6795698/posts/9zXNbPGqm5f)

- **Travel.** No matter where you go, share a post about
  your experience. Almost every place in the world
  holds interest for some people.

The Elements of Google+ Style

With a 100,000-character limit, there's a lot of space to express yourself—or bore people. Let these practices guide
your writing style:

- **Be brief.** The sweet spot for posts is two to three
  paragraphs of two to three sentences each. If in
  doubt, it's better to be too short than too long.

- **Edit.** Hallelujah! On Google+ you can edit a post
  after you've shared it—unlike Facebook and Twitter.

Editing a post after you've shared it.

Don't hesitate to refine, supplement, and correct your posts. (You can also edit the comments you've made on other people's posts.) Not editing your posts and comments is like visiting Hawaii and not going swimming.*

- **Provide a link to the source.** Your expository posts—à la a blog post—might not contain any links to external sources, but when you're acting as a curator, you should link to your source document. The goals are threefold: first, to enable readers to learn more from the document; second, to send traffic to the source as an act of gratitude; third, to increase your popularity by increasing the page count and visibility of others.

- **Use the active voice.** "Apple announced a new iPhone today" is more powerful than "A new iPhone was announced by Apple today." Brevity and the active voice are two sides of the same coin.

- **Include a photo, photo album, or video.** Every post should contain some "eye candy." Including a website link will usually automatically bring in a photo or video. You can also take screenshots or use the images at Wikimedia Commons (http://commons.wikipedia.org) and Flickr Creative Commons (www.flickr.com/creativecommons). There's more information about using photos on Google+ in Chapter 7, "How to Share Photos."

- **Organize with bulleted and numbered lists.** If you're going longer than four paragraphs, use a bulleted or numbered list. This makes grasping multiple points much easier for people. I often decide whether a long post is worth reading by seeing whether it has a bulleted or numbered list.

- **Stylize your text.** Google+ enables you to do a tiny amount of stylizing if you put certain characters on both sides of your text. They are **bold** (asterisk on each side: *your text*), *italics* (underscore on each side: _your text_), and ~~strikethrough~~ (hyphen on each side: -your text-).

- **Add a hashtag.** In Chapter 3, "How to Master Circles and Streams," I explained how to use a hashtag to find interesting content. The flip side is to add hashtags so that other people can find *your* posts. For example, if you're sharing a post about bacon, add "#bacon" to the post.

- **Post regularly.** Share a post at least once a day. Sometimes I share 20 posts in a day, but that's too many for most followers. Three to five posts per day is about right.

- **Give credit.** Acknowledge the work of your sources. The ideal way to do this includes a +mention—for example, "Hat-tip to +Halley Suitt Tucker." Then the person you are crediting will get a notification of your action.

- **Share when your audience is awake.** Sounds simple, but share your posts when your target audience is awake. If your audience is spread around the world, my advice is share posts from 10 a.m. Pacific to 10 p.m. Pacific because that when the spammers in Asia are asleep.

- **Repeat your posts.** My tweets are repeated four times, eight hours apart. I can prove that this increases click-throughs by a factor of 4. However, the Google+ community isn't ready for this much repetition, and it may never be. But I do share a truly useful post such as a PowerPoint template to raise money more than once.

(https://plus.google.com/11237483663409 6795698/posts/MYAxAa6kFhb)

THE MECHANICS OF POSTING

Now that we're locked and loaded with content and we know the right stylistic practices, let's post a message.

First, click on "Share" in the upper-right corner of any Google+ page or the text box on your profile or home page. Then type in your post.

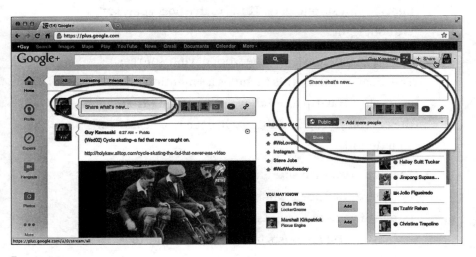

Two ways to get to the text-entry area.

Second, add a photo, photo album, video, link, or location to your post by clicking on the three icons in the bottom-right corner of the text-entry area. The display of these buttons is to prompt you to include a photo, photo album, video, or link on your post.

Here's more information on how these buttons work:

Adding a photo, video, or link.

- **Pictures from phone.** Android and iOS devices running the Google+ application from Google can automatically upload pictures to your album. You access them by clicking on the thumbnails. This feature is called "Instant Upload" because the pictures from your phone have been instantly uploaded to your album.

- **Pictures.** The camera icon enables you to add a picture or an album of multiple pictures. You can also drag and drop a picture into the text-entry area.

- **Video.** The boxed red arrow enables you to search for and add a YouTube video, record a video with a webcam, send a video from your phone, and upload your own video. You can also place a link to a YouTube video in the body of your text, and Google+ will grab the video from that link.

- **Link.** The blue link enables you to include links to websites. As with a link in the body of your text, Google+ will grab a photo from the page and a brief description of the story.

You can only insert a photo, embed a video, or add a link by using these buttons. You can, however, attribute a location to any picture, video, or link.

Alternatively, you can include the link to a video or website in the body of your text without clicking on these buttons, and Google+ will automatically embed the video or preview the website. If you include multiple links in the body of your text, Google+ will embed and preview only the first one.

Next, decide whether to "disable comments" and/or "lock" the post. You won't do this very often, but these features do come in handy. Disable comments when you know that your post is likely to start a comment war because your topic is politics, abortion, or religion. Lock the post—which means that people cannot share it—if you want to limit distribution of the post.

Disabling comments and locking a post.

Fourth, determine whom you're sharing the post with. Remember, there are four ways that circles do this:

- **Circles.** A specific circle or circles.

- **Your circles.** Anyone who is in at least one of your circles.

- **Extended circles.** People in your circles and the people in their circles if you publicly display who you've circled on your profile.

- **Public.** Everyone who has circled you.

You can also share with people in two additional ways:

- **+Mentioning people.** By +mentioning people in the body of the text, you can share a post with them. They do not have to be in any of your circles. If you +mention only the person and do not share the post with any circles or the public, then it's a private message to the person.

- **Including e-mail addresses.** If someone isn't on Google+ yet, you can type "+" or "@" and her or his e-mail address in the post, and Google+ will send the post to the person. (This is a clever way to suck more people into Google+!)

WHAT TO AVOID

Margie Clayman is the director of client development at Clayman Advertising. In a blog post called "12 Most Easy Traps to Fall Into When Curating Content," she explains what *not* to do as a curator. It is a good checklist of practices to avoid, so here is a summary of that post:

1. Curating content only from the biggest bloggers out there.

2. Curating content only from people who are your personal friends.

3. Getting the blogger's name wrong.

4. Expecting a lot of promotion for your efforts. (By this she is referring to expecting gratitude and reciprocity from the article that you promoted.)

5. Only gathering posts that have something to do with you.

6. Gathering posts that are all from the same perspective.

7. Including too much of your own content.

8. Not including enough of your own content.

9. Listing posts with no commentary about why they are there.

10. Making it hard for readers to move between your post and the posts you're curating.

11. Making lots of errors in your write-ups.

12. Making it too hard. (In other words, convincing yourself that curating is hard when it's not that hard at all.)

How to Schedule Your Posts

Post that I share between 7 a.m. and 7 p.m. Pacific time generate the most insightful and engaging comments. Wouldn't it be great to schedule posts that you find after 7 p.m. for the next day?

There is a way to do this by using a Chrome extension called Do Share. It enables you to draft your posts in advance and then set a time for them to be shared. Note, however, that your computer must be on and Chrome running at the scheduled times of the post. If they are not, the scheduled posts revert to being "drafts," and you need to reschedule them.

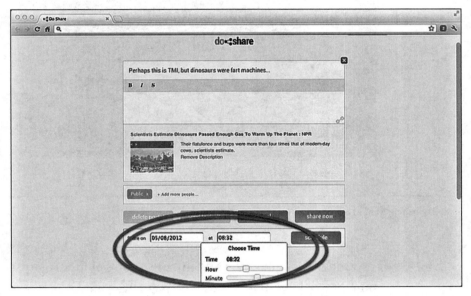

Scheduling a post with Do Share.

SEE THE RIPPLES

Google provides eye candy called Ripples to show how people have shared public posts. Click on the arrow in the upper-right corner of a post and select "View Ripples." You'll see a cool graphic depicting the recent and public shares of your post, including the people who did the sharing. *

Launching Ripples for a post.

Google+ displays the amount of sharing plotted against time underneath the circles (see page 91)—note how sharing usually happens in the first few hours and then dies out. Other information includes a list of major influencers, some statistics about the sharing, and the language spoken by the people who publicly shared the post.

I've found two ways to use the information from Ripples. First, you can circle someone who shared your posts with a large number of people. You might even want to suck up to them. In the screenshot on page 92, for example, the Dalai Lama should circle and suck up to Vic Gundotra. ;-)

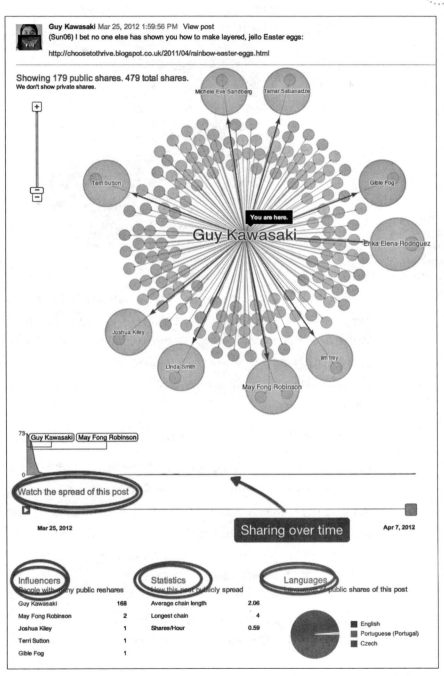

Displaying the ripples of the post.

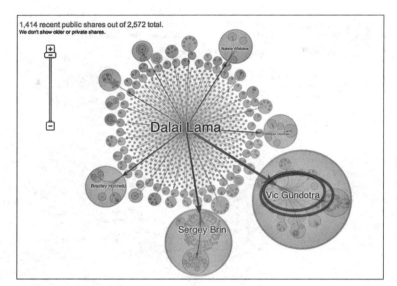

1,414 recent public shares out of 2,572 total.
We don't show older or private shares.

Dalai Lama

Natalie Villalobos

Christian Oestlien

Bradley Horowitz

Vic Gundotra

Sergey Brin

Viewing Ripples for the Dalai Lama's hangout with Desmond Tutu.

Second, you can study the Ripples of other people to see who effectively shares their posts. Then you can circle these *über*-sharers and try to engage them, too. In the example above, if you were studying the Ripples of the Dalai Lama post, you'd circle Vic Gundotra because he has a lot of clout.

HOW TO FIND YOUR MOST POPULAR POSTS

Ripples is cool, but so is a service from Finland called Google+ Suomi (www.googleplusesuomi.com). It displays your most popular posts in terms of +1s, shares, and comments. To use the service (the site is in Finnish as I am writing this book), use the link below and replace my account number (11237483 6634096795698) with yours.

http://www.googleplussuomi.com/timelinetest.php ?googleid=112374836634096795698&sort=share

You can get your account number by clicking on "Profile" in the navigation ribbon on the left side of the window.

This site provides an excellent window into what your readers have chosen as your best posts.

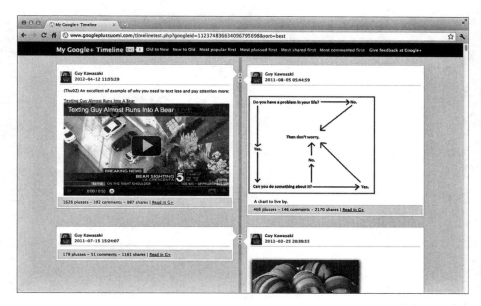

Using Google+ Suomi to view your most popular posts.

Conclusion

One last piece of advice: despite what you read in this chapter, there are no "rules" in Google+ (or any social medium, for that matter). There is only what works for you and what doesn't work for you. Feel free to ignore what I say and "think different."

Additional Documentation on Google's Website

About Ripples

(http://support.google.com/plus/bin/answer
.py?hl=en&answer=1713320)

How to Optimize for Social Search

> *If Edison had a needle to find in a haystack, he*
> *would proceed at once with the diligence of the bee to*
> *examine straw after straw until he found the object*
> *of his search. . . . I was a sorry witness of such doings,*
> *knowing that a little theory and calculation would*
> *have saved him ninety percent of his labor.*
>
> Nikola Tesla, *New York Times*, 1931

THE DAWN OF SOCIAL SEARCH

On January 10, 2012, Google announced "social search integration," and the earth shook a little. This means that when people use Google's search engine, their results encompass Google+ connections.

The theory is that search results are more relevant when they take into account one's social connections. Social search is paradigm shifting. It means that who you know changes what you get (WYKCWYG).

For example, if people who circled me searched for "venture capital," they would see results similar to the screenshot on page 97.* Here's what's going on:

- Fifty posts by my friends and me about venture capital. These might be worth checking out.

- Three promoted links. No problem, Google monetization as usual.

- One Wikipedia definition of venture capital.

- One post by me about venture capital. Since I'm your friend, my posts may interest you.

- In the right sidebar, Google is telling you Mahesh Murthy, a venture capitalist at Seedfund, is a source of venture-capital information.

The integration of Google+ into search results will influence the topics people write about and the quantity of their posts. In this example, I would share more posts about venture capital so that my posts appear in searches and to stay on the list of suggested people in the right sidebar.

If I were Mahesh Murthy, I would share more posts about venture capital for the same reasons. If I were another venture capitalist trying to enhance my visibility or that of my firm, I would get my butt on Google+ in order for my posts and profile to appear in Google's search results—call this SED: Search Engine Duhism.

Turning off social search yields results like the one shown on page 98—in other words, the way results looked before integrating Google+ into search but with one big exception. Look at the right sidebar: Google is still promoting people to check out on Google+ even though social search is turned off.

Finally, regardless of whether social search is turned on, if you scroll to the bottom of the page, you can share a Google+ post to the public or your circles. This is an easy way to ask a question of your followers, as shown on page 99.

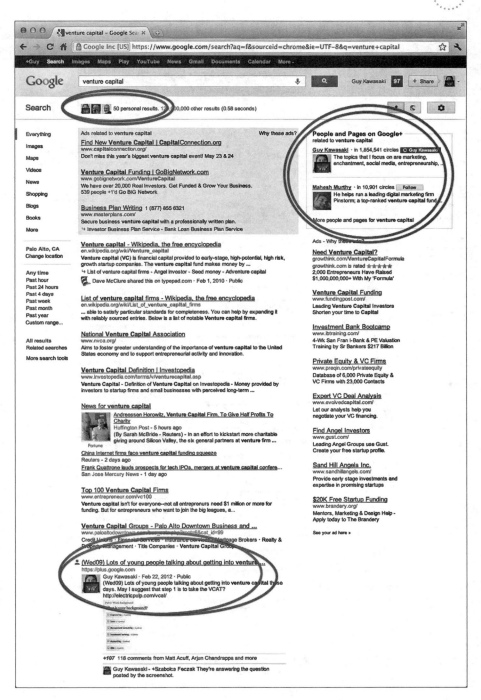

Searching for "venture capital" with social search turned on.

Searching for "venture capital" with social search turned off.

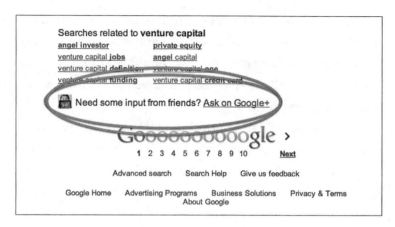

A convenient way to ask your friends about a topic.

VIS-À-VIS FACEBOOK AND TWITTER

Let's compare social search to how you would search for "venture capital" before the advent of social search. First, you'd Google the term and find the usual stuff. Then you might search Facebook to see if any of your friends are involved with the topic. The results would show people, fan pages, and then updates about the topic, but not the deeper, reference-based type of results that a Google search provides.

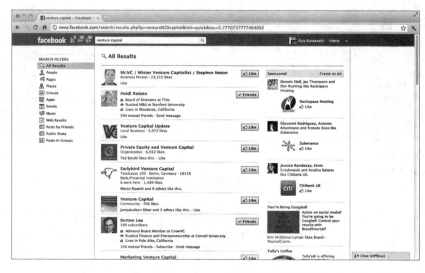

Searching Facebook for "venture capital."

In other words, a Google search with social search enabled can provide better results in one step than the two-step, two-sites (Google plus Facebook) method. And the Google search will also get better and better as more of your friends join Google+.

If you searched for "venture capital" on Twitter, you'd get real-time uses of the term in tweets plus people who use the term in their profiles as well as videos and pictures. The usefulness of a Twitter search is dependent on your goal—if it is to find breaking news and perspectives about venture capital, then it can be useful. However, searching Twitter is not useful for reference information.

Results of searching Twitter for "venture capital."

ANOTHER EXAMPLE

I love social search so much that I want to provide another example of how it makes life better. Suppose you're a fashionista, and your "Super Bowl" is Fashion Week. BSS (before social search) you would simply search for "Fashion Week" in Google and find the usual results for the Mercedes-Benz Fashion Week home page as well as coverage by the usual magazines.

Now ASS (get your mind out of the gutter; it stands for "after social search"!) you would see the Google+ "Fashion Week" results: 40 mentions of the people you've circled and my post of the 42 Fashion Week photos collected by the Big Picture. Your social connections would probably provide a very different perspective of the event, and you'd see the photos that they took with their phones. And you'd still see the usual search results after the social results.

Searching for "Fashion Week" with social search.

It's going to be a long time before people use Facebook or Twitter as a search engine. Two things would have to happen. First, Facebook and Twitter would have to add reference results like those you'd find in Google. Second, millions of people would have to alter the reflexive action of "Googling" something and use Facebook or Twitter instead.

Conclusion

Social search should bring a smile to the face of every marketer because this is one of the few comprehensible ways to influence search results: post stuff about a topic, and you'll probably be included when your friends search for the topic. Social search means goodness for all: searchers get more relevant and valuable search results and "searchees" know how to appear in those results.

Additional Documentation on Google's Website

Google Social Search

 (http://www.google.com/insidesearch/features /plus/index.html)

How to Share Photos

> *My portraits are more about me than they are about*
> *the people I photograph.*
>
> RICHARD AVEDON

INTRODUCING DAVE POWELL

Dave Powell of ShootTokyo (http://shoottokyo.com) wrote this guest chapter. He is a photographer and blogger from Boston, Massachusetts, who has lived in Tokyo for the past 11 years. He focuses (no pun intended) on photos from Japan, and he is one of the most popular photographers on Google+. He uses a Leica M9—that alone makes him a badass. Now, over to Dave.

PEOPLE THINK VISUALLY

Every post you make on Google+ should include a picture or video because you are competing for people's attention in an overloaded world. Great photos evoke emotions, ask the viewer questions, and draw people to read what you have written.

If you are posting a link to a website, Google+ will do most of the work by pulling in a picture. If you don't like the choice it has made, you can click the little gray arrows at the upper-left corner of the image to scroll through other available images from that website or click the "X" to remove what Google+ pulled in and upload your own picture by clicking on the gray camera icon which turns blue when your pointer is over it.

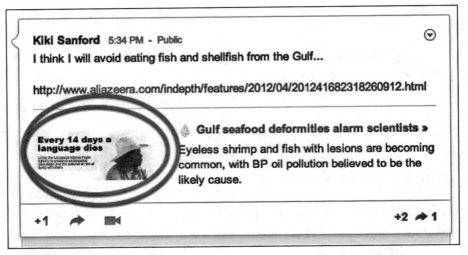

An automatically pulled-in picture: "Every 14 days a language dies" has nothing to do with Gulf seafood deformities.

Sometimes the website that you're linking to won't have a picture—or the picture sucks. Then you have to take a screenshot or find another picture that illustrates your post. In a pinch, here are two solutions. First, you can take a screenshot of the logo or name of the website. That's better than nothing.

Second, you can search through the pictures at Wikimedia Commons or Flickr Creative Commons to find one to use. Be creative. For example, if you're writing a post about Australian politics, you could use Wikipedia's map of Australia or the Australian flag.

Regardless of how you find a picture, remember that if something is worth writing about, it's worth illustrating with a picture.

GETTING YOUR PICTURES READY TO UPLOAD

The vast majority of people use smartphones and point-and-shoot cameras to take pictures for Google+ and other social-media sites. Serious photographers do three things using their photo-editing software before they share their pictures—you don't need to do this, but just in case you want to know:

- **Size.** Resize your photos for their ultimate, optimal use. I always upload my images at 1,800 pixels wide so people can use them as desktop backgrounds.

- **Metadata.** Fill out the "metadata" with keywords so search engines can find your image. If you took a photograph of Tokyo Tower, then tag the image as "Tokyo" and "Tokyo Tower." Google can't actually "see" your image, so help it with metadata.

- **Copyright information.** Embed your copyright information: the year, your name, and "All rights reserved." I state that it is OK to use my images for noncommercial purposes. I also embed contact information so that people who want to use them commercially know how to reach me. Read the Google terms of service for information about how Google handles content rights.

HOW TO UPLOAD PICTURES

There are three primary ways to upload photos for your Google+ posts:

- **Manually.** You can click on the gray (which turns to blue) camera icon and upload a picture or create an album. This is the way most people upload photos to Google+. It is easy and fast. You can also drag and drop a photo into the text-entry area.

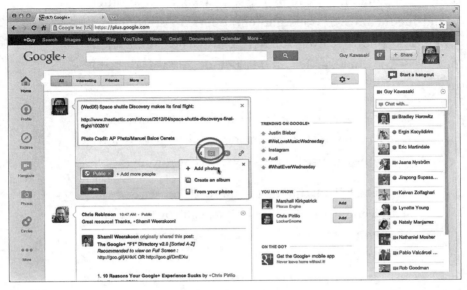

Manually uploading a picture.

When you sign up for Google+ you automatically get a Google account and your photos are accessible from other Google services such as Blogger and Picasa Web Albums. Then when you manually upload a photo via a post, your image is placed in an album called "Photos from posts." This makes it easy for you to quickly upload photos, but it might make it difficult if people want to browse your other photos on a specific topic.

- **Picasa.** You can upload your images directly to the Picasa album and share the album on Google+ by clicking on "Share." Picasa will choose the image in the upper-left corner as the image seen in your stream in Google+. You can reorder the images under "Actions."

The benefit of uploading directly to Picasa is that you can choose the folder for each photo. For example, when I want to share another photo from a trip to China, I put it in the China album and share the entire album. This enables viewers to see all of the images together.

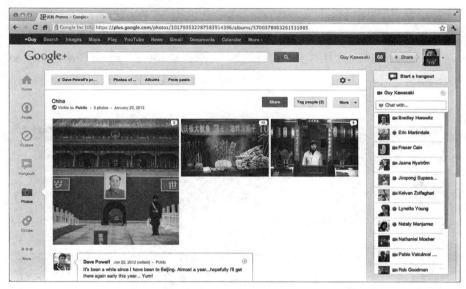

Using a Picasa album.

- **Google+ application on phones and tablets.** If you take a photo using the Google+ app, and it's syncing with Google Photos, the photo will automatically upload from your phone to your Google+ album. Then you can share your photos without having to download them from your phone or tablet to your computer.

VIEWING AND EDITING UPLOADED PICTURES

To see a full-screen version of a photo in Google+, you simply click on it. If the photo is in a post by another person, you have two additional options. First, you can hit the space bar to hide the comments and see a less-cluttered view of the picture.

Second, you can click "Options" in the bottom-left corner to download a full-size copy of the image (if the owner of the image enables this capability) or view information about the image such as the camera used, shutter speed, aperture, and focal length. (Google automatically pulls in this information from photos. It's not necessary to enter it.) You can also report the photo and/or report a comment on the photo to Google+ in case it is inappropriate.

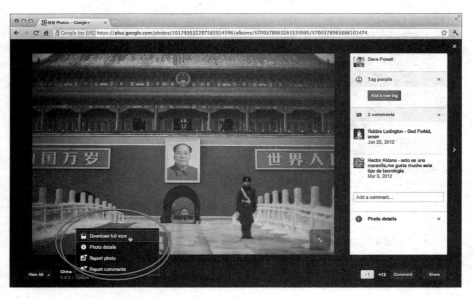

Clicking on "Options" yields four actions.

If the photo is in your post, you can also use an online photo editor called "Creative Kit." You get to it by clicking on "Creative Kit" in the upper-left corner of the window. * Then you'll see a window like the one shown at the top of page 109.

The Creative Kit enables you to enhance your photo using basic techniques such as cropping, exposure adjustment, and color correction, as well as adding text. Google also

Launching the Creative Kit.

Using the
Creative Kit.

provides thematic special effects such as hats, spiders, and
ornaments during holidays such as Halloween or Christmas.

You might want to see a larger version of a photo but not
necessarily a full-screen one. To do this, install a Chrome

extension called +Photo Zoom, and you can hover your cursor over an image to see a larger version of it.

Using +Photo Zoom to enlarge pictures.

THE BIG PICTURE

After using Google+ for a week or two, click on "Photos" to look at the totality of your Google+ pictures.

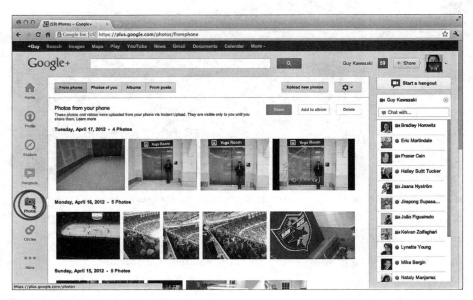

Accessing your photos.

You'll see a page with these five choices to access all the photos you uploaded as well as all the photos that people have "tagged" you in.

- **From phone.** These are the photos that your phone or tablet automatically uploaded.

- **Photos of you.** You'll find three sections: "Is this you?" "Photos of you with …," (which displays the photos that you've been tagged in with others), and "Photos you've been tagged in" (where people have tagged you alone).

- **Albums.** These are the albums that you created from multiple photos.

- **From posts.** These are the photos that you've manually uploaded to your posts. The photos that links brought in automatically are not included.

NAME-TAGGING ZEN

Seeing the collection of "Photos of you" can be disturbing because it looks like people can follow your activities. Google is aware of this problem, so it offers some options:

- **Control whose name tags of you are automatically approved and who can download your photos.** You must approve name tags before they are linked to your profile. However, the name tags of people you've circled are approved by default. You can control who can approve a name tag and who can download your photos by going to your Google+ settings.

- **Approve or deny name tags.** Click on the "Photos" icon, click on "Photos of you," and then click on the check mark to approve of the name tag or the "X" to disapprove it. You can also block the person who tagged you from ever tagging you again.

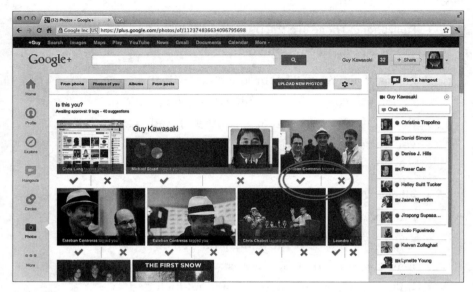

Approving tags.

- **Remove existing name tags.** As the screen on the next page shows, click on the "Photos" icon, click on "Photos of you," click on the photo in question, find your name in the right sidebar, click on the "X" to revoke approval, and click "OK" to confirm.

If none of these methods takes care of your problem, complain directly to Google. Its employees are extraordinarily helpful.

PHOTOGRAPHY TIPS

Cameras, even the ones in your phone, are remarkably powerful and sophisticated devices these days. Here are a few ways to take better photos for Google+:

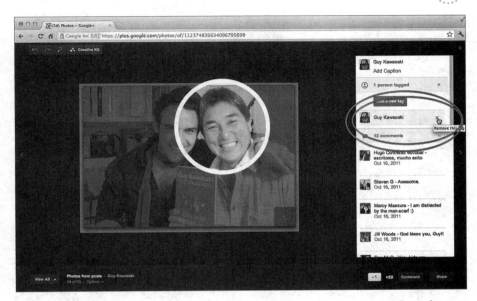

Removing a
name tag.

- **Know your camera.** Nothing will improve your
  photography more than knowing your camera. Get
  out and practice, practice, practice.

- **Compose your photo.** Good composition will do more
  for your photograph than anything else. First,
  use leading lines to draw your viewer into your
  photograph as shown on page 114.

  Second, think of your picture as a grid of two
  horizontal and two vertical lines that divide it
  into nine equal boxes. Place your subject at the
  intersection of any of these lines, not dead center—
  this is called the "rule of thirds."

- **Fill the frame.** Make the subject of your picture
  fill the frame. What really matters when you are
  photographing people? Most of the time it is their

An example of
leading lines
(photo credit:
Dave Powell).

face, their smile, and their eyes. Get in close and fill 80 percent of the frame with their face. Review the corners of the frame and make sure you only have objects relevant to your picture in the frame.

- **Watch your backgrounds.** Nothing ruins a great photo more than a busy background that distracts your viewer, so fill the frame and ensure that the background is simple, clean, or even out of focus.

- **Change perspective.** For example, when you are taking photos of your children or your pets, get down and take the image "at their level" and "from their perspective." It will make your images far more interesting.

- **Be thoughtful.** Don't post photographs that could embarrass someone or yourself. Remember: the Internet doesn't have an eraser. Don't post images you do not want your mom, dad, husband, wife, kid, or future boss to see.

- **Start a 52 or 365 project.** If you want to improve your photography, take a picture once a week or once a day. There are lots of groups doing this on Google+ that you can observe. For example, there's a very structured 52 project called GPLUS::P52::2012. You can also search for the hashtag "#creative366project" (366 for a leap year), and you will find many people doing daily photo projects.

(https://plus.google.com/u/0/107553450680914912872/about)

If you observe these recommendations and put a little more effort into your photos, more people will probably read your posts.

Photo Profile Settings

Things can get pretty tricky with photos and privacy, so Google has implemented several controls. To customize these settings, go to your Google+ Settings.

Photos

☐ Show photo geo location information in newly uploaded albums and photos.

☐ Allow viewers to download my photos

☑ Find my face in photos and prompt people I know to tag me. Learn more

People whose tags of you are automatically approved to link to your Profile:

[○ Interesting ×] [○ Friends ×] + Add more people

When a tag is approved, it is linked to your profile, and the photo is added to the "Photos of you" section.

You can change the visibility of your photos and videos tabs on your profile.

Settings for photos.

By using these settings you can determine if your geographical location is displayed as well as whether people can download your photos. "Find my face in photos and prompt people I know to tag me" is powerful. If you turn it on, Google+ will build a model of your face. Then when you or someone you know encounters a picture that matches the model, Google+ suggests tagging you in the photo. The final setting enables you to control whose tags of you are automatically approved.

Conclusion

Google+, more so than Facebook and Twitter, is photo oriented. Invest the time to find or create good photos for your posts, and you'll reap the benefits of more followers and more engagement with your followers. This, in turn, will make Google+ an enjoyable experience for you.

Additional Documentation on Google's Website

Photos

(http://support.google.com/plus/bin/answer.py ?hl=en&answer=1047374&topic=1257351&ctx =topic)

How to Respond to Comments

> *Honest criticism is hard to take, particularly from a*
> *relative, a friend, an acquaintance, or a stranger.*
>
> FRANKLIN P. JONES

YOUR SWIMMING POOL

During the first few months after going live, Google+ was a beautiful swimming pool filled with enchanting people making substantial, supportive, and serene comments. Then all hell broke loose on September 21, 2011, when Google+ opened for anyone to join. Overnight, posts were inundated with clueless, crass, and commercial comments.

This has made many people angry, crazy, and nostalgic about the "good old days" of the summer of 2011. However, comments indicate that people are reading your posts—even if they are spammers. (I explain how to deal with spammers later.)

I deal with approximately two hundred comments every day on my posts. I read almost every one of them because I want to engage as many people as possible. If you are not responding to comments, you are not truly tapping into the power of Google+. This involves lots of work, but it will pay off for you.

NOTIFICATION ZEN

In order to respond to comments, you need to find them. There are three ways to do this. First, you can manually monitor your posts for new comments. This involves checking your posts several times after you share them.

Second, you can pay attention to the red number in the upper-right corner of the Google+ bar to see your notifications. When you click on that number, you'll see notes about who commented on your posts, shared your posts, +1ed your posts, circled you, and messaged you.

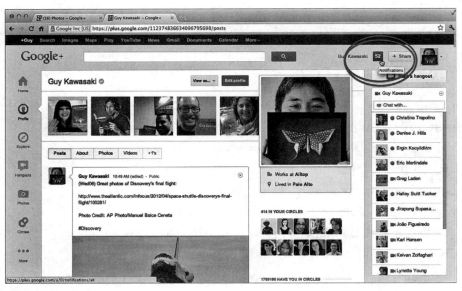

The number of pending notifications.

Third, you can tap Google+'s e-mail notification system. You'll see that as you share more posts, the manual method and the "red number" methods can involve a great deal of work. Also, if people make reference to you in other posts all over Google+, the manual method would leave gaping holes in your awareness.

Fortunately, Google+ enables you to control who can interact with you and how you receive notification of these interactions. First, click on the "Home" button in the navigation ribbon on the left side of the window and then select "Settings" by clicking on the gear icon on the right side of the window. On the Google+ Settings page, you can customize who can interact with you. At the beginning, I would let anyone interact with you. You can always tighten this up later.

Who can interact with you and your posts

Who can send you notifications? Learn more   `Anyone ⬍`

Who can comment on your public posts? Learn more   `Anyone ⬍`

Who can start a Messenger conversation with you?   `Your Circles ▾`

The next settings section enables you to add text-message notification to your phone. My volume of notifications is so high that I don't want to constantly receive text messages, so I don't use this feature.

Determining who can interact with you.

Phone: `▲ Edit phone number`

Edit where you want notification sent to. Your public profile will be discoverable by your phone number.
View SMS Terms

Country   `United States ⬍`

Mobile Number   +1 `[          ]`

Verification Code   `Send verification code`

Cancel

via ⦿Push notifications ◯SMS ◯Don't notify me

▾ Add SMS security PIN (optional)

Adding text-message notification via your phone.

Finally, you can determine which activities generate a notification e-mail. There are four options:

- **"Mentions me in a post."** When a person has +mentioned you in a post, you'll get an e-mail. I recommend turning this on because a person who went to the effort of +mentioning you deserves a response.

- **"Shares a post directly with me."** This is as close to person-to-person e-mail as Google+ gets because it's a way to directly send you a post. However, it can get dubious because it's also a way for spammers and creeps to contact you. Start with it on, and see if works for you.

- **"Comments on a post I created."** This means that whenever someone comments on your post, you'll receive notification even if it isn't a +mention. To start, you won't get many comments, so this is OK. However, as you gain more followers, you may get too many notifications this way.

- **"Comments on a post after I comment on it."** This notification will let you know that you should revisit a post because someone made a comment after you made a comment. The thinking is that someone responded to you, so now you should check back to see whether you need to respond again.

Note that the choices you make in the Phone column control your mobile phone's notifications settings.

You can also turn off notifications for specific posts. For example, there may be many comments in a post by a popular person. If you add a comment too, everyone else's comments will appear in your stream for a long time. You can "mute" a post to prevent this, and you will no longer see the post.

Receive notifications

Notify me by email or SMS when someone...

Posts	Email	Phone
Mentions me in a post	☑	☑
Shares a post with me directly	☐	☑
Comments on a post I created	☐	☑
Comments on a post after I comment on it	☐	☐
Circles	Email	Phone
Adds me to a circle	☐	☐
Photos	Email	Phone
Tags me in a photo	☐	☑
Tags one of my photos	☐	☐
Comments on a photo after I comment on it	☐	☐
Comments on a photo I am tagged in	☐	☐
Comments on a photo I tagged	☐	☐
Shares a photo with me, that I might be in. Learn more	☑	☐
Messenger	Email	Phone
Starts a conversation with me	☐	☑
Communications about Pages	Email	Phone
Receive updates and tips that help me get the most out of my Pages	☑	☐
Learn about the latest changes, enhancements and new features	☑	☐
Learn about related Google products, services, events and special promotions	☑	☐
Participate in surveys and pilots to help improve Pages	☑	☐
Receive invitations to manage Pages	☑	☐

Choosing which actions generate notifications.

Muting a post so that you no longer see it.

After much experimentation with these methods and settings, I've settled on the following practices:

- Respond to everyone who +mentions me anywhere on Google+. Notification via e-mail is a godsend for doing this.

- Manually check my recent posts for people who have not +mentioned me, but who merit a response. Fortunately, 90 percent of comments happen within the first two hours of sharing a post.

- Never mute any posts. I figure that putting in hours of effort is the price one has to pay to succeed on Google+.

E-mail Notification Responses

When you receive notification of +mention in your Gmail inbox, click on the e-mail, and you'll see that it contains the post—not just a link to the post. Without clicking on the link to go to the post on the Google+ website, you can reply to comments from within the e-mail.

This is an awesome feature. It makes responding to comments much more efficient which in turn increases the engagement level of Google+.

The Tao of Responses

Over the course of using Twitter and Facebook—and now Google+—I've developed this approach to responding to comments. Admittedly, I don't always adhere to my own advice, but this is what I try to do:

Responding to a comment via a Gmail e-mail.

- **Have fun.** By responding to comments, you can transcend "pushing" and "broadcasting" and engage in an actual two-way conversation. I have fun with my comments because the banter on Google+ is usually funny, interesting, and often insightful.

- **Clean the pool.** Deleting and reporting are a kind of response too. I delete inappropriate comments (profanity, racism, and off-topic rat holes) and report spammers with great impunity. In other words, unlike any other social media service, on Google+, you can dictate your own "terms of use." You'll learn more about this in Chapter 11, "How to Deal with Bozos."

- **Respond fast.** You should respond within two hours of posting because few people read and comment on posts that are much older than that. This also means you should share posts when you have time to monitor comments—think "fire and follow" not "fire and forget."

- **Think Twitter, not *War and Peace*.** Resist the temptation to answer comments on a point-by-point basis. Just synthesize the gist of the comment and respond to either the major point or the point you want to respond to. If someone asks five questions, this doesn't mean you need to write five answers.

- **Consider the total audience.** The audience for your response is everyone who will read it—not just the commenter. This is different from private e-mail in which the recipient is all that matters. Others are watching and judging, so act accordingly.

- **Stay positive.** Since others are watching, you should stay positive and pleasant. You can never go wrong by taking the high road. In doing so, you may "lose the battle but win the war" for credibility and popularity with the rest of your readers.

- **Ignore orifices.** You can pretend you never saw a disagreeable comment. There's so much action on Google+ that people are never sure if you've seen their comment. Plus, ignoring a comment may irk the orifice more than if you responded in an argumentative way.

- **Agree to disagree.** Believe it or not, there isn't always a right and a wrong or a best way. In these cases, you can agree to disagree—even if you know your commenter is wrong and you're right. Life is too short to be doing battle all the time, and most battles are not worth fighting.

- **Smoke 'em.** On the other hand, you'll find instances where a comment is so outrageously racist, misogynist, or biased that the right thing to do is bury the person. This rarely happens—again, I get about two hundred comments per day, and I tell people off about once a month.

Conclusion

Remember that your posts are your swimming pool. You can do anything that you want. If you don't like profanity, delete. If you don't like bigotry, delete. If you don't like sexism, delete. The goal is building and maintaining an enchanting presence—not exemplifying free speech.

Additional Documentation on Google's Website

Notification

 (http://support.google.com/plus/bin/answer
.py?hl=en&answer=1054277&topic=1257350
&ctx=topic)

How to Hang Out and How to Chat

> *The old ways are dead. And you need people around*
> *you who concur. That means hanging out more with*
> *the creative people, the freaks, the real visionaries,*
> *than you're already doing.*
>
> HUGH MACLEOD, *Ignore Everybody*

WHAT IS A HANGOUT?

Google+ provides live video conferences called a "hangout." There are three kinds of hangouts. First, the "regular" ones where up to 10 people can participate. Hangouts enable you to conduct a group online video conference, chat via text, share a document, share desktops, and watch YouTube together. Many people love them because it brings Google+ relationships to life with live sound and video, and they are voyeuristic in a cool way. *

Second, **"Hangouts with extras"** includes the capability to name a hangout, share a whiteboard, and invite telephone participants.

Third, there are **"Hangouts On Air"** that lets you live broadcast to an unlimited number of people. Google automatically records these hangouts as YouTube videos. You can learn more about hangouts on air here.

(http://services.
google.com/
fh/files/blogs/
Hangouts_On_
Air_Technical_
Guide.pdf)

Alida Brandenburg making the "+" sign during a Table for Ten hangout.

To show you the power and coolness of hangouts, here are some YouTube recordings compiled by Michael Delgado:

- **Table for Ten.** Ten people cooking the same recipe at the same time. [There's even a website dedicated to cooking called ChefHangout (www.chefhangout .com).]

(http://www.youtube.com/ watch?v=Xiak3tXThxo&hd=1)

- **Trey's Variety Hour.** Photographer Trey Ratcliff with friends.

(http://www.youtube.com/ watch?v=fWapWoVW7RE)

- **ENGL5060 at Texas Tech.** An online writing class analyzing a paper.

 (http://www.youtube.com/
watch?v=OlJKKalYG7Y&hd=1)

WHAT YOU NEED

You don't need much to do a hangout: a computer with a web camera and microphone, plus something to say; that's about it. You can also use a smartphone with a front-facing video camera to join a hangout but not to start one. (Technically, you can participate in hangouts without this equipment by using only the text chat feature, but this defeats the purpose of a hangout—it's like buying a Macintosh to run MS-DOS.) As a rule of thumb, if you can do a Skype video conference, you can do a hangout.

In a post called "How to Promote a Book Using G+ Hangouts," Kevin Kelly, "senior maverick" and former executive editor of *Wired*, provided a great list of ways to make hangouts work. Here's a summary:

- Designate one person as the organizer, boss, and host.

- Cap the length at one hour.

- Start with everyone introducing him- or herself so people feel included.

- Encourage shy people to speak up—they may have the best things to say.

- Invite people to the hangout five to ten minutes before the scheduled start so they can set up their systems.

- Encourage people to use headsets and earphones so everyone can hear better.

To Kevin's list, I would add three recommendations:

- Encourage people to place the light source in front of their faces so everyone can see them better.

- Suggest that people look at the web camera, not the faces of the participants on their computer screen, to make eye contact.

- Request people who are not speaking to mute their systems to reduce background noise.

If people don't have a web camera or smartphone, they can dial into the hangout to listen to the conversation, but only listening to a hangout seems to defeat the purpose, if you ask me.

STARTING A HANGOUT

Starting a hangout.

To start a hangout, go to your Stream and click on "Start a hangout" in the right-hand sidebar.

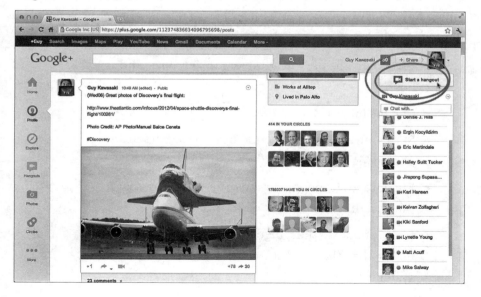

Then you determine what circles and individuals to invite to the hangout, name the hangout, and decide if the session will be a "Hangouts on Air" (public for anyone to watch and recorded for YouTube). You can also restrict minors from participating and try a "hangouts with extras."

A post will appear in the stream of the people you invited. It will also list the people who are currently in the hangout. If 25 or fewer people are invited, they will receive a notification—that is, the red number in the upper-right corner of the window will increase by 1. Theoretically, you're paying attention to that number, so you click on it, see the notification, and join the hangout.

Setting up a hangout.

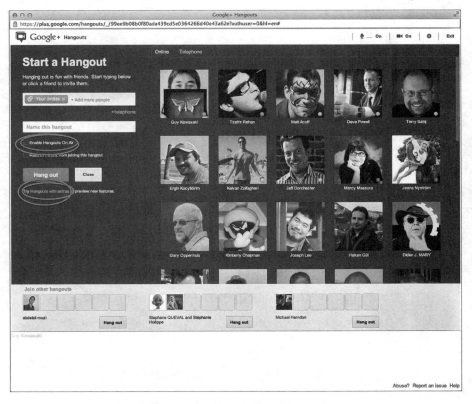

You can also start a hangout by clicking on "Hang out" in the area above the comments in a post and from a chat

Starting a hangout from a post.

window. You would do this when the impetus for a hangout is a particular post or comment.

FINDING OTHER HANGOUTS

People are using hangouts for more than, well, simply hanging out with friends. People are teaching meditation, learning languages, holding press conferences, interviewing job candidates, and providing customer service.

Until you get the hang of hangouts, you can join other people's hangouts. The Google+ community has created many resources to help you find public hangouts.

Websites

- GpHangouts (http://gphangouts.com)

- Hangoutlists (www.hangoutlists.com)

- Plus Roulette (http://plusroulette.com)

Chrome Extensions

- Hangout Canopy

- MyHangouts

Google+ Page

- Google Shared Calendars

(https://plus.google.com/117173351243749913463/posts)

Here are people who use hangouts in powerful and interesting ways whom you can look up and circle:

- Daria Musk (Music)

- Sarah Hill (News)

- Fraser Cain (Science)

- Mike Elgan (Tech)

- Thomas Hawk (Photography)

- Ray Sanders (Astronomy)

TEN IS THE LONELIEST NUMBER

Hangouts can reach more than 10 people if you "broadcast and record" them. This enables people to watch and listen to hangouts but not participate. Hangouts can also be recorded and made available on YouTube. Google calls this "Hangouts on Air" and is rolling it out to users over time. You can watch

Dalai Lama, Desmond Tutu, and a few thousand friends hanging out.

how the Black Eyed Peas, the Dalai Lama (with Desmond Tutu!), and The Muppets used this capability on YouTube.

Privacy and Control

As you can imagine, live video and audio can yield some nasty privacy and decency issues, so here's how privacy and control work in hangouts:

- Even if you started the hangout, you don't "own" it. Any participant can invite others to join it.

- There isn't a way to kick anyone out of a hangout, although *you* can leave at any time.

- You can block someone during a hangout, but he won't be kicked out immediately. Neither of you will be able to hear or see each other during the rest of the hangout, and everyone—including the person—will know that you blocked him.

- The person you blocked cannot join future hangouts that you're in, and Google+ will inform him that someone in the hangout had blocked him.

- You cannot join hangouts that contain a person you've blocked.

- If people obtain the link to a hangout that they weren't expressly invited to, they can still get in.

CHAT

Chatting is a little old school, but it's still very useful. You can use it for low-bandwidth moments such as using GoGo on a Virgin America flight or when staying at a $400/day four-star hotel and paying $12.95 for Internet access.

There are two forms of chat: video and text. Unlike a hangout, a video chat is with only one other person—like Skype not on steroids. Text is what you'd expect: a window where you and one other person type back and forth. You can chat with "anyone you have a relationship with" on Google+, Gmail, iGoogle, Google Talk, and Orkut. If you don't see someone in the list, type his or her name in the search box above the chat list.

Starting a chat.

The green icon between the person's picture and name represents what type of chat will work with the person. A green circle means text only. A green movie camera means video. A red movie camera means the person is busy, and a yellow movie camera means the person's computer is on, but it's idle. You can alter your chat settings by clicking on the downward pointing arrow to the right of your name.

Futzing with chat settings.

CONCLUSION

Google+ hangouts blow away what you can do on Facebook and Twitter. It's one of those "enabling technologies" that people can use to "let a hundred flowers blossom." If you're feeling like a Google+ evangelist, you could use hangouts as a kind of Trojan Horse by telling your friends to just use hangouts and to stick with Facebook and Twitter for everything else. Soon you'll be seeing a lot more of them on Google+.

Additional Documentation on Google's Website

About Hangouts

 (http://support.google.com/plus/bin/answer.py?h
l=en&answer=1215273&ctx=cb&src=cb&cbid=14
zkydw9oe1t8)

Chat

 (http://support.google.com/chat/?hl=en&topic=17
25163#topic=2386431)

10

How to Get More Followers

> *Try not to become a man of success but try rather to become a man of value.*
>
> ALBERT EINSTEIN, *LIFE*, May 2, 1955

ARE YOU A LIAR?

There are two kinds of people on social networks: those who want more followers and those who are lying. (Social-media "experts" hate when I say this because they don't have many followers.) Let's be honest: gaining more followers is the acid test of social media because it shows whether you are interesting, intelligent, and cool.

People either circle you or not. They either keep you in a circle or not. How awesomely simple, pure, and democratic. Ignore the experts when they say quality is more important than quantity—the more followers you have, the richer your Google+ (and Facebook and Twitter) experience.

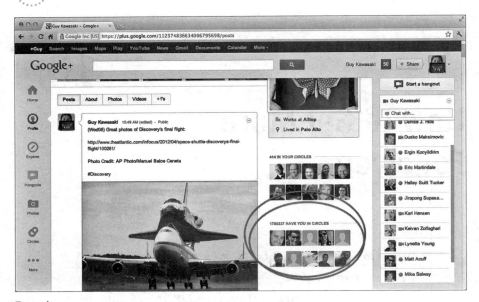

To see how many people have circled you, click on the "Profile" icon and look on the right side of the window.

WAYS TO ATTRACT MORE FOLLOWERS

Are you with me, or are you a liar? If you're with me, here are ways to gain more followers:

- **Perfect your profile.** At HotOrNot.com people decide whether they want to meet others by looking at their pictures. At eHarmony people complete an extensive questionnaire along 29 dimensions of compatibility. Google+ is more like HotOrNot than eHarmony: you have a few seconds to impress a person who's looking at your profile.

  The difference between a great profile and a mediocre one is approximately an hour of work. Make the investment. Go back and reread Chapter 4, "How to Make an Enchanting Profile," for tips on how to create a hot profile.

- **Share good shiitake.** Life is simple: share good stuff; people will spread the word, and you'll get more

followers. Everything else is optimization. Refer
to Chapter 6, "How to Share Posts," for a complete
discussion of this topic. Your goal is to write such
good shiitake that people won't want to ever miss a
post.

- **Share in public.** Don't hide your good stuff under a
  bushel. If you want followers, you need exposure
  and awareness as far and wide as possible. For
  example, if you found a great article about knitting,
  share it with your knitters' circle as well as the
  public.

- **Add the Google+ badge to your website and blog.**
  Doing this provides an easy way for your
  visitors to click on "Badge" and go to your
  Google+ profile. Learn more about the Google+
  badge here.

(https://
developers.
google.com/+/
plugins/badge/)

- **Compile a thematic circle.** According to Fraser
  Cain, the guy who shared the science circle,
  there's no better way to gain followers than to
  compile a great circle of people in a particular
  category. Include yourself in the category
  (assuming you're relevant to it!), and then share
  the circle. As people add the circle to their
  collection of circles, you'll gain followers too.

- **Help people.** At any moment, somebody on Google+
  can use your help. For example, if someone needed
  dining advice for a trip to Hawaii, I'd tell him that
  you don't have to drive to the other side of Oahu to
  find great shave ice. Wailoa Store is one mile from
  Waikiki, and its shave ice is as good as Matsumoto
  Shave Ice. Here's a power tip: Google makes

everyone an expert, so even if you don't know where the best shave ice is in Hawaii, you could probably figure it out with one minute of effort and look like an expert.

- **Make meaningful comments.** Meaningful, insightful, and "inciteful" [sic] comments can help you attract more followers. I've seen many cases where a comment is more interesting than the post itself. That's a good goal. Read Chapter 5, "How to Comment," to review how to make good comments.

- **Respond to comments in your posts.** Respond to 100 percent of the comments that require answers. Not every comment does, but people want to engage with people who are responsive. This makes responding to comments one of the best ways to prove that you're a good person and thereby gain followers.

- **+Mention others.** Always use a +mention when referring to anyone else on Google+. I'm getting tired of telling you this, but it will make you more visible to the community.

- **Give credit.** When others point you to something that you share, acknowledge them with a +mention. This simple action shows that you have class and that you are an insider who knows how the game works. You'll also rack up karma points, so ABC: "Always Be Crediting."

- **Invite people to join.** One way to be popular at a party is to invite your friends to it. This principle works on Google+ too, so invite friends to the service, add your Google+ profile link to your e-mail signature, and talk up Google+ among your friends and family. If they won't follow you, who will?

- **Participate in hangouts.** On February 10, 2012, approximately 100 Google+ members met up in person in New York City. Most of them didn't know one another six months earlier. Hangouts brought them together—the event was even called NYC HIRL (Hangouts In Real Life). Try hanging out to make new friends and add followers.

(https://plus
.googlecom
/101432770
709896418
691/posts/Z
7LzAxoa3ZA)

- **Help Google+.** If I were not on the Google+ list of suggested people to follow (http://plus.google .com/getstarted/follow), I would not have nearly the number of followers that I do. To get on this list, you have to be a huge celebrity or a big help to Google+—or both. I can't help you become a celebrity, but I can explain how to help Google+: deliver new members, content, and street cred. If you do this, you might get on the list too. That's the only reason I'm on this list.

SHALLOW ME

I love watching the number of my followers increase. Google+ can send you a notification when people circle you, but I don't do this because, ahem, there would be too many notifications. You might find it fun to receive notifications, though, so change your Google+ settings to make this happen.

Receive notifications		
Notify me by email or SMS when someone...		
Posts	✉ Email	📱 Phone
Mentions me in a post	☑	☑
Shares a post with me directly	☐	☑
Comments on a post I created	☐	☑
Comments on a post after I comment on it	☐	☐
Circles	✉ Email	📱 Phone
Adds me to a circle	☐	☐

Turning on notification for when people circle you.

My goal for my reputation is the kind of sentiment that PE Sharpe shared about me:

> *I rarely re-share posts from the so-called Big Dogs on G+, but +Guy Kawasaki remains one of my favourites. When I arrived on G+ during field and beta I had no idea who he was; I just knew that he consistently shared posts with an underlying sensibility that appealed to me. He was also one of the more approachable big dogs. It was a wild ride during those first months— I felt completely out of my depth amongst the testosterone and HDR-driven technocrati—but Guy was consistently generous in interacting with his many followers, myself included.*

How to Get More Page Views and +1s

Along the lines of getting more followers, increasing traffic to your website or blog may also interest you. To do this, Google enables you to add a "G+Share" button and "+1" button for your visitors.

When visitors click on the "G+ Share" button, they are able to share a web page or blog post the same way people can share a Google+ post, including adding commentary and selecting circles. So by adding this button, you'll increase page views of your web properties. Learn more about the "G+ Share" button here.

(https://
developers.
google.com/+/
plugins/share/)

You can also add a "+1" button. Then visitors can +1 your website pages and blog posts. These +1s are a ranking signal and *may* affect the ranking of the pages and posts in Google search results. Only Google insiders know what +1s really accomplish and what they will accomplish in the future. But it's so easy to add the "+1" button to your web properties that you have nothing to lose by doing so.

The journey from lunch to landfill [video]

Posted Apr 25th, 2012 at 12:46 PM and seen 541 times

Anything on your lunch plate that does not end up in your belly eventually makes its way to the landfill (or China). Los Angeles public radio station KPCC tracks your trash's journey from garbage can to dumpster to sorting facility to landfill in an informative video that might make you think twice about the garbage you produce at every meal.

👍 3

Like

Send

14

Tweet

G+ Share

Share this on Google+ as Guy Kawasaki

Share

1

Share

Waste less by going green.

Annie Colbert

0 responses

Sharing a website article.

Conclusion

While I don't advocate an obsession with the number of people who follow you on Google+, it is a useful indicator of the quality of your participation. Generally, the more followers you have, the more rich and rewarding your Google+ experience, so try a few of the methods I've explained in this chapter.

How to Be a Little Fish in a Big Pond

> *There's a fine line between fishing and just standing*
> *on the shore like an idiot.*
>
> STEVEN WRIGHT

INTRODUCING PEG FITZPATRICK

Peg Fitzpatrick wrote this guest chapter. She is the director of marketing and social-media manager for Kreussler Inc., a partner of re:DESIGN, and a managing partner of 12 Most (http://12most.com). After she read a draft of this book, she thought that I didn't fully appreciate the challenges that "regular people" encounter when they join Google+, so I put the ball in her court and told her to write something that fixes the problem. As my mother used to say, "You're either part of the problem or part of the solution."

THE GUY KAWASAKI REALITY-DISTORTION FIELD

The problem with Guy is that he doesn't realize that his visibility and notoriety are tremendous advantages. Succeeding on Google+ for him and people like Robert Scoble is easy.

But what if you were a regular Joe or Josephine? How can you make Google+ work for you? Here are the 12 most powerful tips to succeeding on Google+:

1. **Don't expect to be an overnight success.** Even if you have a following on Facebook and Twitter, these people may not be on Google+. If they are, they may not make the effort to find you, so you will need to find them. Getting discovered by new people takes even longer. There's no easy way around this.

2. **Pay your dues.** Social media takes effort—every day! You need to create or find great content to share. Invest the time it takes to make good posts on Google+. Slapping up a link often creates an unappealing post of just text that few people will notice. People are much more likely to notice a pretty post and act upon it.

3. **Watch and learn.** Unsure about how to share and comment? Watch how popular people do it. Guy's advice to me when I was hesitant to comment on posts was, "Get over it." Once I started commenting, my Google+ experience was totally transformed. Google+ flows like a combination of Twitter and Facebook, so you are in a new environment but not so new that you can't get the hang of it.

4. **Be original.** I love this quote by Oscar Wilde: "Be yourself, everyone else is taken." This simple reality seems to be lost on many folks in social media as they "borrow" content from others. As you are analyzing styles and observing, it's great to learn, but also develop your own original style. People can spot a copycat, and they won't respond to your content when they see it is not true to you.

5. **Experiment with different content.** People use each network—Google+ (passions), Facebook (people), and Twitter (perspectives)—for different reasons, so they have different expectations for the type of content they'll see. Be willing to try new things, and don't expect that the content that has been popular with your followers on Google+ will be as popular on Twitter or Facebook. Don't get frustrated because the recipe you posted on Facebook isn't popular on Twitter and your blog isn't shared all over Google+. Adapt and grow with each platform.

6. **Change how you interact.** Interaction is different on Google+, but in a good way! Conversations are truly conversations, not just "thank you for the retweet" or an @mention for your blog being tweeted. Unless it is just a message that someone circled you, notifications indicate that someone took action, and you should reciprocate. There is much less gratuitous chatter and more "meat" on Google+.

7. **Have fun.** Somewhere along the way many people started focusing on Klout and other metrics and forgot that social media is supposed to be SOCIAL! "Social," according to Dictionary.com, is "seeking or enjoying the companionship of others; friendly; sociable; gregarious." Don't be afraid to post something that is entertaining or funny—social media is a diversion for many people who just want some inspiration or a laugh.

8. **Jump in with both feet!** OK, so you are on Google+, it's time to stop watching and start engaging! Be generous with the +1s, sharing, and commenting. Those features are there for a reason. No one else

can get your feet wet but YOU! You will find that people are ready to engage and are looking for interesting and smart people. Let that be you!

9. **Stay involved with your other social-media channels.** When you are a little fish, you need to keep swimming in all the ponds. You can use your traffic on other channels to redirect some of it to Google+. People tend to like their existing social-media platforms (usually Twitter or Facebook), and they are hesitant to try something new such as Google+. So teach your friends and family how to use Google+, and be the bridge between new and old.

10. **Don't compare yourself to the big fish.** Comparing yourself to people like Guy will just make you feel bad. Part of the reason that the big fish get so many comments is that folks want to say they "know" them. Big fish have lots of people who have circled them, and more people will see their material. People will search for them by name. Don't begrudge someone who worked hard and has more followers—instead, accept that you have some work to do, and do it!

11. **Be confident.** You might wonder whether anyone is seeing your posts. Rest assured that someone is. Don't share stupid messages such as "Is this thing on?" or post woe-is-me comments about how you aren't getting any traffic. This is very unattractive and isn't going to win you any fans. This is an instance where the "fake it till you make it" rule applies. Assume that fabulous, smart people are reading your material, and post accordingly.

12. **Be kind, humble, and helpful.** Being nice to others opens many doors. Helping people is a great way to make new friends, and they will remember that you were kind. Sharing your talents with others reinforces your positive social-media experience. People can spot a fake or a person with a big ego a mile away. If Guy can be humble, so can you.

Conclusion

Remember: social media is an individual endeavor and works differently for each person. Put the time into learning what you need to know and making friends. You will find that soon enough everything will fall into place, and you may even blow past Guy.

How to Deal with Bozos

> *There is nothing worse than aggressive stupidity.*
> JOHANN WOLFGANG VON GOETHE

GOOD NEWS, BAD NEWS

Metcalfe's law states that the value of a network is proportional to the square of the number of connections in that network. Robert Metcalfe, a researcher at Xerox PARC, originally applied this observation to Ethernet nodes, but now people use it to describe the usefulness of belonging to a service such as Facebook, Twitter, and Google+.

Kawasaki's law states that the number of bozos in a service is proportional to the square of the number of people in that network. This means that the more popular Google+ becomes, the more bozos you'll encounter. Bozos come in these recognizable forms:

- **Schmexperts.** These elitists consider themselves "experts" and appoint themselves as arbiters of the right way to do everything. They are, in short, schmucks + experts. (Hat-tip to Bill Meade for coining this term.)

- **Idiots.** Idiots share spammy links to sites that you'd never use and write comments that make no sense for the post. They are most active between 10 p.m. and 6 a.m. Pacific—this is why I hardly post during these times.

- **Trolls.** Trolls deliberately try to provoke anger, rage, and other antisocial emotions. Mostly men, these are your run-of-the-mill mama's boys, perverts, and harassers. They hide behind a Google+ profile and act out weird fantasies that titillate some part of their adolescent lizard brain.

- **Bigots.** These clowns look for fights in topics such as politics, religion, and abortion. They cannot conceive of alternate perspectives, but they want you to adopt theirs. There's mostly downside if you interact with them.

YOUR ARSENAL AGAINST PEOPLE

You can ignore the posts and comments that you don't like. This involves no customization or clicking on your end and is effective if you enjoy reading some posts from a person but not others. In this case, skim the person's posts and train yourself to ignore what you don't like. To misquote Thomas Gray, "Ignoring is bliss."

If you want to take your actions up a level, you have three options: removing from your circles, blocking the person, and reporting the person. *

- **Removing.** One way to deal with bozos is to remove them from your circles. This means that you won't see their posts though they can still see and comment on yours. Google+ is like a cable or satellite channel—if you don't like its programs, cancel your subscription.

- **Blocking.** Blocking is a "restraining order" on people so that they get out of your face. This works, for example, with an ex-boyfriend, ex-husband, or ex-employee. Several things happen while they are logged into Google+.

  - They cannot see your public posts.

  - You cannot see their content in your stream.

  - Google+ removes them from your circles as well as your extended circles (circles of the people you've circled)

  - They cannot make new comments on your posts. However, old comments remain, so you'll have to manually delete them.

  - They cannot see your comments in other people's posts.

  - They cannot +mention you in posts and comments.

- **Reporting.** You can report a person who consistently acts inappropriately, and Google might suspend that person's account. If you want a person out of your Google+ experience but don't necessarily want Google to suspend the account, just block him instead.

There are two ways to invoke these actions against people. First, you can use the Circles editor by clicking on the "Circles" button in the vertical navigation ribbon in the left sidebar. Then select the circle the person is in, and do your thing.

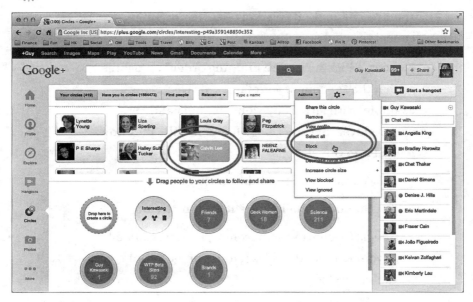

Blocking people using the Circles editor—though I would never block Calvin Lee.

Second, you can perform these actions as you encounter people. Click on their name to go their profiles, and click on "Block" or "Report."

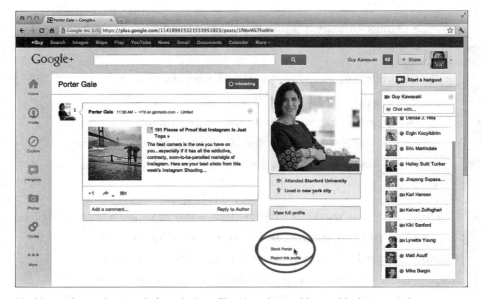

Blocking and reporting people from their profile—though I would never block Porter Gale.

YOUR ARSENAL
AGAINST COMMENTS

You can also take actions against specific comments (as opposed to the people themselves). First, you can "Delete comment." Here are the kinds of comments that I delete from my posts:

- **Nonsensical characters.** These look like someone typed a bunch of random keys on his computer.

- **Profanity.** Set your own tolerance level for your stream. In my case, I delete anything stronger than "shit."

- **Spam.** One sign of increasing popularity on Google+ is that you'll attract spam. These are comments with promotional links to sites that have nothing to do with your post.

- **Inappropriate sentiments.** I've posted links to photo essays about earthquake victims and received comments such as "they deserved it." These comments are so insensitive that I delete them.

- **Personal attacks.** Parody is cool. Sarcasm is cool. But mean-spirited, personal attacks are over the line in my stream.

- **Off-topic remarks.** I delete comments where someone is trying to hijack a topic. For example, if I share a message about Macintosh, and the comment is about global warming, it's gone.

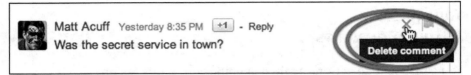

Deleting a comment—though I would never remove a comment by Matt Acuff.

Be sure to use Google Translate for Google+ or something like it to figure out what people are saying when they comment in other languages. This is a fabulous tool that enables people who don't speak a common language to carry on a simple conversation.

Don't worry that you might offend people by deleting their comments. First, it's unlikely that they'll even notice. Second, it's your stream to manage how you want. I have deleted hundreds of comments and have not received any complaints.

REPORTING AND BLOCKING COMMENTS

The second action you can take on specific comments on your own posts is to "Report abuse or block." This is an appropriate reaction to spam, profanity, and harassment. You are removing the comment from the view of others and telling Google that it should suspend the account, and you can also block the person while you're at it.

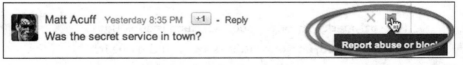

Reporting abuse or blocking a comment on your own post. Again, I wouldn't do this to Matt Acuff.

If other people "Report abuse or block" a comment on your post or if Google determines that a comment is spammy, the comment will disappear from view for everyone else. This is Google cleansing your stream of comments.

Google has
hidden posts
that are
spammy.

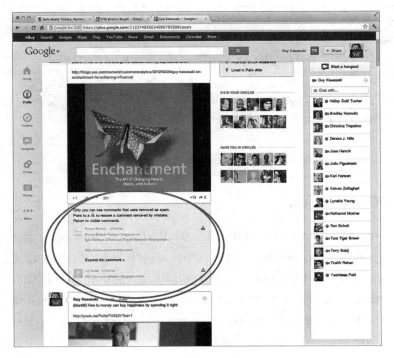

Viewing the
hidden posts.

The control of spam and inappropriate comments is one of the most fluid areas of Google+. Procedures have changed several times during the writing of this book. Suffice it to say that Google is well aware of the issues here and is on your side in the battle against spammers, bozos, orifices, and trolls.

NUKE 'EM

In two clicks a Chrome extension called "Nuke Comments" enables you to delete a comment, report the person who made the comment, and block the person. If you are really bold (I am!), there's even a way to do this with one click. This Chrome extension is second only to Replies and More as a method to improve the Google+ experience. If you want to get rid of crap very quickly, Nuke Comments will change your life.

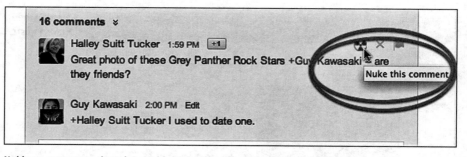

Nuking a comment—though I would never nuke a comment by Halley Suit Tucker.

CONCLUSION

In the old days (summer of 2011), there were a lot fewer people on Google+ and therefore a lot less bozosity. Those days are gone—and never to return. The good news is that there are now a lot more interesting people on Google+. The bad news is that you have to learn a few techniques to deal with the bozos who have joined.

Additional Documentation on Google's Website

Blocking

(http://support.google.com/plus/bin/
answer.py?hl=en&answer=1047934)

Ignoring

(http://support.google.com/plus/bin/answer
.py?hl=en&answer=1619779&topic=1347964
&ctx=topic)

How to Thrive in the All-Boys' Club

> *At their core, women fear that men will kill them. At*
> *their core, men fear that women will laugh at them.*
>
> GAVIN DE BECKER, *The Gift of Fear*

INTRODUCING LYNETTE YOUNG

Sometimes women freak out when strangers circle them on Google+. They consider this invasive, creepy, and just short of stalking. Not being a woman, I asked Lynette Young, the creator and curator of Women of Google+ (www.womenofgplus .com), to empower women to optimize their use of Google+ by writing this guest chapter. Here's Lynn.

WHAT REALLY MATTERS

There are more women than there are men using social media, except on Google+. Why? One theory is that Google+ first opened by invitation only in June 2011, and mostly Google engineers invited people to join. Since most of the engineers were men, they invited their friends, also men, and unintentionally skewed the population toward males.

Another popular theory is that Google+ is too hard for women to understand, being technology and all—as crazy as this may sound! True or not, both theories spurred me to create the Women of Google+ community.

The very best way I made Google+ work for me was to circle people who shared my interests, passions, and ideas. Guy once said, "Google+ is the place to find the people I want to know and connect with that share my passions." When I first joined Google+ I made it a priority to use the platform in a new and different way from how I used Twitter, Facebook, and LinkedIn.

I sought out and circled professional women, and specifically women in technology and the sciences. If your passion is music, photography, food, parenting, engineering, or cat herding—regardless of gender—seek out people with similar interests and engage them.

It doesn't matter how many men or how many women are using Google+ or social media. What really matters is that every person finds value from participating. Sadly, women are more prone to online harassment and trolling solely because of their gender. This is not the case for everyone, but it is something to watch for when interacting on any social network, even Google+.

Take Control of Google+

Don't let fear control you. We cannot control how others act, but we can control how we respond. Thankfully we have amazing tools and resources within Google+ to help us mold and control our own experience. This is my advice on how to make your Google+ experience a great one:

- **Take charge of your Google+ experience.** You are in charge of the people you circle, the content you post, and the content you consume. Do not follow people out of a sense of obligation or etiquette. Do not change or alter what you publish to appease "your audience." If others are unhappy with your content, they are free to uncircle you. And you too can uncircle people who post content you don't like. Your Google+, your rules. Period.

- **Treat the block function as your BFF (best friend forever).** Guy explains a lot of this in Chapter 11, "How to Deal with Bozos." When I first had the need to block someone in Google+, I actually felt bad about it. In the end, not once have I received a complaint from someone that I blocked.

- **Manage people's ability to interact with you.** The best defense is a good offense. Being proactive about who you let share, download, and comment on your posts goes a long way to prevent whack-jobs from bugging you. For example, I let anyone comment on my posts but not comment on or download my photos . Why? I was growing weary of deleting "u r so preeeeety" and "sexy lady, nice smile, follow me?" comments. Maybe the comments were harmless, but leaving them only leads to trouble. Restricting people's ability to interact has drastically reduced the amount of cleanup and troll hunting I had to do.

- **Do not feed the trolls.** Yes, it's hard—even the best of us have cooked a gourmet meal and hand-delivered it to them. The new kind of troll is cleverly disguised as an interested, intellectual person who just has a different point of view. As soon as personal attacks and harassment starts, you should delete, block, and report. It's the only way to deal with them.

- **Don't freak out.** If you encounter trolls or other unsavory people, stay calm. Even if it seems like a personal attack, it's not. It is just insecure people hiding behind the Internet who are trying to make themselves feel superior. Keep calm and decide what you want to do. Delete, block, and report. Once you clear them out of your view, you can go on enjoying the intelligent and amazing Google+ community.

- **Be aware of your surroundings.** Walking down a dark street alone at night has its safety risks. So does participating in Google+ hangouts. Be aware of your background, as it appears through your webcam and the conversations that can be heard through your microphone. During some hangouts, I could read the team jersey of people's kids in photos in the background. Unless I know every participant in a hangout, I shut my door and make sure I have a curtain up behind me. Besides, I don't want people to know how messy my bookcase and shelves are.

CONCLUSION

The overwhelming majority of people using Google+ have an *enchanting* and valuable experience with the community.

Don't let a few bad apples ruin a perfectly amazing adventure! Focus on the positive—the vast majority of people on Google+ are cool, caring, and friendly.

And visit the Women of G+ website (www.womenof gplus.com) and circle our Google+ page for a truckload of positivism. We maintain great resources for women to enhance their Google+ experience including a directory, a newsletter, events, editorials, and tutorials.

(https://plus
.google.com/
10828529663
2855004171/
about?hl=en)

How to Avoid Cluelessness

> *The whole problem with the world is that fools*
> *and fanatics are always so certain of themselves,*
> *but wiser people so full of doubts.*
>
> BERTRAND RUSSELL

STEVE "JOBES"

I used to meet people all the time who claimed to know Steve Jobs and pronounced "Jobs" as if it rhymed with "robes." They also said that they really liked "'Frisco." For the record, if you don't want to look clueless, Steve's name rhymes with "mobs" and locals refer to San Francisco as "the City."

The goal of this chapter is to help you avoid looking clueless on Google+. And, by grokking these seven principles, you'll also be able to spot clueless people, which will help you decide who's worth paying attention to.

- **Telling people how to share posts.** Even though I wrote a chapter about how to share posts, a sure sign of cluelessness is telling other people how to use Google+. There are few, if any rules. The number one rule is "Do what works for you."

- **Announcing that you're no longer following someone.**
  No one gives a shiitake who you uncircled. This is
  equivalent to standing up in a high school cafeteria
  and announcing that someone is no longer your
  friend. If you no longer care what someone says, just
  stop following the person and get on with your life.

- **Asking people why they uncircled you.** Changing the mix
  of one's circles is a constant process on Google+,
  so don't panic when people uncircle you. Arguably,
  if you ask why and grovel, you'll lose even more
  followers. Just keep posting, commenting, and
  responding, and let people self-select.

- **Asking people to circle you.** People seldom ask others
  to circle them on Google+—unlike on Twitter, where
  it happens all the time. Let's keep it this way. If you
  want more followers, earn them with the quality of
  your posts. If Groucho Marx were alive today, he'd
  say that anyone who asks you to circle him or her
  isn't worth circling.

- **Selling something with every post.** You can accuse me of
  many things but not of hypocrisy: Google+ is a great
  way to promote your product, service, or website.
  No problem. You'll look clueless, however, when
  you try to sell something too frequently. Take it from
  someone who does a lot of promotion on social
  media services: no more than 5 percent of your
  posts should be a sales pitch.

- **Writing in ALL CAPS.** By this time, everyone should
  know better than to write in all caps, but it still
  happens. God made uppercase and lowercase

letters, so use them both. This makes your posts much more readable.

- **Calling yourself a guru or expert.** If you are one, people will know. If you aren't one, no one is going to believe your self-description. In particular, a "social-media guru" is an oxymoron. Nobody really knows how to use social media yet—it's just that some people try to charge for advice, and some don't.

CONCLUSION

Clueless people represent a small percentage of the Google+ population. Keep this in mind because it may seem like Google+—and even the world—is filled with clueless people. This is simply not true, so don't let these bozos taint your Google+ experience. Social media, and Google+ in particular, enable you to discover new people, new things, and new ways of thinking.

How to Get Google+ Help

> *You can't help someone get up a hill without getting closer to the top yourself.*
>
> H. NORMAN SCHWARZKOPF

YOU'RE NOT ALONE

The probability that you're the only person who's encountered a particular problem on Google+ is near zero. The probability is also near zero that no one can figure out how to do something that you want to do. So when you find yourself in these situations, here's what you should do:

- **Check Google+'s Help Center.** Google has thoroughly documented how to use Google+ (www.support .google.com/plus). This is your first line of defense.

- **Make contact with the Google+ support community.** This is called "Google+ Discuss." You will find many knowledgeable users and Google employees there who will be happy to help you.

 (https://productforums.google.com /forum/#!forum/google-plus-discuss)

- **Circle the Google+ page.** Google maintains an official Google+ page. It is a good source of news and tips.

 (https://plus.google.com/u /0/101560853443212199687 /posts)

- **Ask Google's community managers.** Google has a small cadre of community managers who foster the use of Google's various tools such as Chrome, Gmail, and Web Search. Here's a list of these gurus (www .recommendedusers.com/google-community -managers).

- **Contact an expert.** The Google+ community is remarkably egalitarian, flat, and non-hierarchical, so share a public post with a +mention of an expert. You'll be amazed that many of them will jump right in and help you with your issues. You can spot an expert because she usually has tens of thousands of followers, though this is not an infallible assumption.

- **Follow the Google+ Tip hashtag.** There's a group of caring people who constantly share tips on how to use Google+. To stay on top of their wisdom, search for this hashtag: "#Googleplustip" (http://plus .google.com/s/#Googleplustip).

- **Circle Google+ Updates.** This is a Google+ account that shares posts about changes to Google+. To learn about the latest features of Google+, circle "Google+ Updates."

(https://plus.google.com/u
/0/110415663864880023628
/posts)

- **Read the Official Google Blog.** This blog covers all
  Google activities, but you can read only the articles
  that pertain to Google+ to lessen your load.

(http://googleblog.blogspot.com/search/label
/google+)

- **Ask your Google+ followers.** With as little as a few
  dozen Google+ followers, you'll probably get all
  the assistance you need by asking for help. Don't
  hesitate to do this for fear of embarrassment or
  infringing on relationships.

     Google+, and social media in general, is a way
  to learn from others as well as demonstrate your
  expertise. Also, it's OK to ask for help, because it
  enables your followers to repay you for posting good
  stuff. I ask for help from my followers all the time—
  for example, to beta-test this book. Blow me away:
  241 people volunteered!

- **Ask your Twitter and Facebook followers.** This may seem
  odd, but many of your followers are on multiple
  services, so asking a Google+ question on Twitter or
  Facebook will probably work.

- **Ask on Quora.** Quora is a community-driven website
  where people pose questions and receive answers

from "the crowd." There is a high-quality Google+ forum on Quora. You can give those folks a shot too.

(http://www.quora.com /Google+?q=google%2B)

- **Check the Google+ blogs.** You probably won't find the answers to your specific questions exactly when you need them on Google+ blogs, but they are a good way to stay on top of changes. The easiest way to stay on top of these blogs is Google-Plus.alltop (http:// google-plus.alltop.com).

- **Look for Chrome extensions.** Programmers on Google+ have done a lot of good work to enhance the service. Check out the extensions they've created by searching the Chrome webstore. Also, here's an article about Firefox add-ons and Greasemonkey scripts.

(http://googleplus.wonderhowto.com/how-to /use-firefox-add-ons-and-greasemonkey-make -google-perfect-0131162/)

- **Join the developers' forum.** If you are a developer of Google+ products, then join the Google+ Developers forum. There you can learn about Google+ APIs and plug-ins.

(https://groups.google.com/forum/?from groups#!forum/google-plus-developers)

- **Ask me.** As a last resort, send me a public message, and I'll try to help you. If I can't help you, I'll ask my followers to get the answer. If they can't help you, then no one can.

Help for Developers

If you're a programmer and want help with developing Google+ products, here are resources for you:

- **Google+ Platform** (https://developers.google .com/+/).

- **Google+ Platform Developer Policies** (https:// developers.google.com/+/policies).

- **Google+ Developer Group**

   (https://groups.google.com/forum/?from groups#!forum/google-plus-developers)

- **Support** (https://developers.google.com/+/support).

- **Best practices** (https://developers.google.com/+ /best-practices).

- **Blog** (http://googleplusplatform.blogspot.com/).

- **Downloads** (https://developers.google.com/+ /downloads/).

- **Release Notes** (https://developers.google.com/+ /release-notes/).

CONCLUSION

As my mother always told me, "You don't get if you don't ask," so never be afraid of asking for help on Google+. My prediction is that you'll almost always find the help you need, and you'll make new friends in the process too.

CHAPTER 14

How to Master Google+

> *A timid person is frightened before a danger, a coward during the time, and a courageous person afterward.*
>
> JEAN PAUL RICHTER

EXTRA CREDIT

Writing this book was tricky because I had to balance brevity and completeness. I don't want to give you the impression that Google+ is complicated, but I do want to make you aware of its many cool features. So think of this chapter as extra credit, or recommended reading.

HOW TO USE GOOGLE+ SHORTCUTS

Google+ has several keyboard shortcuts to help you navigate your stream and your profile:

Keystroke	Action
J	Move down one post and selects it
K	Move up one post and selects it
Enter	Moves cursor to comment area when a post is selected. You can tell a post is selected because there's a blue line along its left vertical edge.

Keystroke	Action
Enter + Tab	Posts the comment
Space bar	Move down a screen
Space bar + Shift	Move up a screen

HOW TO USE EVENTS

Events provides the capability to invite people to parties, meetings, and hangouts using Google+. Here's how you do this:

1. Click on "Events" in the navigation ribbon on the left side of the window.

2. Click on "CREATE EVENT."

Creating an event.

3. Select a theme by clicking on the forward and back arrows next to "Change theme."

4. Input your event title, date, time, location, and details.

5. Invite people by +mentioning them, using your circles, or inputting their e-mail address.

Once you send the invitation, your guests will receive an invitation in their timeline. If you used an e-mail address, your guest will receive an e-mail invitation.

HOW TO CONDUCT A POLL

It's fun to conduct quick and simple polls on Google+. For example, as I was writing this book, I ran a poll to see if people thought I should continue to number my posts. (I explain why I number my posts later in this chapter.) By a vote of 172 to 71, people thought that I should.

Polling using +1s.

I know there are ways to embed polls in posts, but why use a sledgehammer when a flyswatter will do? Here's how you can run a quick poll like this one:

1. Write your question, and then include text along the lines of "+1 your choice in the comments below."

2. Share the post.

3. Add comments on the posts that are choices. Do this quickly. You don't want anyone else to comment before you.

4. Disable comments on the post.

5. Watch the +1s tally up.

Disabling comments in a post.

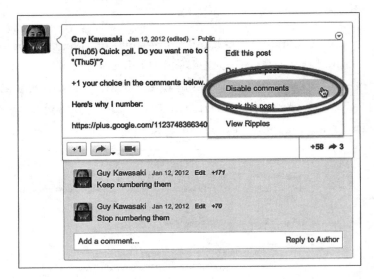

I learned this technique from Robert Scoble, but he learned it from someone else. I asked my followers who invented it, and within minutes, Pradeep Das told me that the start of these Google+ polls was probably this post by Dain Binder. In other words, Google+ is good for fact-checking too.

(https://plus.google.com
/112374836634096795698
/posts/8tJs1a6wxnt)

(http://www.dainbinder
.com/2011/07/how-to-conduct
-poll-on-google.html)

How to Optimize Your Posts for Search Engines

You may read, or someone may tell you, that you need to "optimize your social-media efforts for SEO (search engine optimization)." Let me translate this: it means you're supposed to write your posts and do other tricks in such a way that Google will display your posts higher in search results.

There are several things wrong with this advice. First, you're probably using social media for fun, so you're not trying to optimize search results, click-throughs, and visibility. Therefore, you don't care about search engine optimization.

Second, if you do care, many SEO techniques are closer to witchcraft (and wishcraft) than science. The people (Google employees) who know what Google is doing aren't explaining what it's doing. From the outside looking in, trying to decipher Google's search algorithms is like reading tea leaves in a toilet bowl ... as it's flushing. With the lights off.

Google is in the business of finding the best content and providing it to people. It employs thousands of the smartest people in the world and has spent billions of dollars to make this happen. All you have to do is create good content and let Google do its job.

So whether you're writing for Google+, Twitter, Facebook, LinkedIn, a blog, or a website, personally or professionally, the only SEO advice you'll ever need is:

Write. Good. Shit.

(This is one of those once-a-year times where profanity is OK.)

How to Use Pages

A Google+ "page" is a Google+ account for an organization as opposed to a person. However, the effective use of Google+ by a brand isn't all that different from what you've learned in this book. I'm the guy who boiled down SEO to three words. I can do the same for organizations using Google+:

Implement. This. Book.

This means that the person or team running a Google+ page should act as if they are one person who has read and internalized this book. Step one is as simple as:

- Make an enchanting profile.

- Share posts that add value.

- Trust and be trusted.

- Include pictures and videos.

- Always be commenting and responding.

- Use +mentions.

- Promote no more than 5 percent of the time.

With regard to promotion, I suggest the "NPR model." NPR puts out so much great content that it has earned the right to run a telethon every few months to ask for donations. Your organization should similarly earn the right to promote your products and services by providing great content.

Finally, avoid the common mistakes that spell doom for the use of social media by organizations. I call them the 3Ps:

- **Pretension.** Don't think of your social-media actions as hoity-toity branding, marketing, and positioning. Enjoy yourself as you help people learn about and use your products. Don't get all "corporate" and don't start believing you're doing the rest of us a favor by maintaining a page on Google+.

- **Paranoia.** Just because you encounter a few unreasonable, angry people, don't assume that everyone is like this. And when you take special care of some people, don't assume that everyone will find out and expect the same treatment. I've never seen a social-media faux pas that didn't blow over: people still fly on United even though it breaks guitars, and I'll bet they'll still "race for the cure" at Susan G. Komen events. The worst mistake is to avoid social media because you're afraid something might go wrong.

- **Permission.** Don't be stupid, but don't check with your legal department or management before you do every little thing. The right approach to lawyers is "this is what I want to do, now tell me how I can do it without going to jail" and the right approach to management is to "ask for forgiveness, not permission."

HOW TO CROSS-POST

The odds are high that you already have a Twitter, Facebook, and LinkedIn account. What if you want to share a post on multiple services in order to reach multiple constituencies? The brute-force way is to manually share on each service.

The problem with brute force is that it takes a lot of time—akin to the extra effort that it takes to send separate e-mails to individual recipients rather than one e-mail to multiple recipients. The way around this is to share a Google+

post that automatically posts to Twitter, Facebook, and LinkedIn, too.

If cross-posting appeals to you, then you have to add functionality to Chrome via Chrome extensions. (Note: when Google changes, Google+ extensions often cease to function until they are revised.) Here are three Chrome extensions that enable people to share across services.

- **Streamified.** This enables you to share on Google+ and have your post appear on Twitter, Facebook, and LinkedIn. It will also display your Twitter, Facebook, and LinkedIn streams inside your Google+ stream.

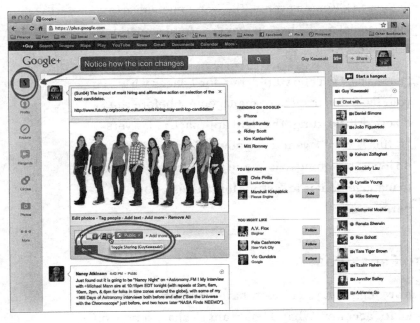

Cross-posting with Streamified.

- **Extended Share for Google+.** This enables your post to appear on Twitter, Facebook, and LinkedIn as well as other services such as Digg, Blogger, Yahoo, StumbleUpon, Technorati, and Netvibes, to name a few. It does not display streams from other services in Google+, however.

- **G+Twitter for Google+.** This enables you to view your Twitter stream, tweet from Google+, share Google+ posts on Twitter, and answer/retweet tweets from Google+.

Unfortunately, there isn't a way for most people to share from Facebook or Twitter to Google+ because Google has not opened up Google+ to accept cross-posts from other services. This is a bummer, because then people who post from Twitter or Facebook to Google+ would see that Google+ is where the action is.

One exception to the unidirectional nature of cross-posting: some members of the Hootsuite Enterprise (http://hootsuite.com/enterprise) program can post to Google+ pages, Facebook, Twitter, and other services at the same time. However, this is only for Google+ pages, not personal Google+ accounts.

Alas, most extensions are only for Chrome, so if you use another browser, you won't have the same selection to choose from. I switched from Firefox specifically so I could use Chrome extensions—such is the depth of my love of Google+.

Here's one possible catch when posting from Google+ to Facebook: "social-media experts" claim that Facebook ranks a post coming through another service as "less good," so it makes the post visible to fewer people. One theory is that Facebook is a possessive and jealous lover, so if you're in Google+ and share to Facebook, it feels jilted and punishes you.

No one, other than the folks at Facebook, knows whether this is true, but it's something to consider. I don't think about it anymore because the extra effort to manually share exceeds the risk that Facebook will punish me. Facebook is a free service, so I don't complain. If someone invites you to dinner at her house, you don't complain that she isn't serving the kind of food you like.

How to Use Google+ on a Phone or Tablet

Google has created applications for Android and Apple iOS devices. These applications enable you to share posts, upload pictures and video, receive updates, and even view posts from people who are in the same area. You can find information about them at this site:

(http://support.google.com/plus/bin/topic
.py?hl=en&topic=1248781)

Most of my posts are crafted on a computer and not posted by phone or tablet. The exception to this is when I take a photo and want to post it with a minimal amount of text—for example, a great meal. When you're out and about and want to post a picture immediately, the Google+ application running on your phone or tablet is the way to go.

If you have an Android or Apple phone or tablet, be sure to install the Google+ app. You'll find it useful to stay on top of your stream and to share posts from remote locations. You can download the Android version or the Apple version and use it in minutes.

How I Share

My sharing process is complex, labor-intensive, and time-consuming, and that's why it's the last topic in this book. You

Google+ app
running on
an Android
phone.

don't need to do most of what I do. However, many people have asked me to explain how I share posts, so here goes:

1. Find good stuff using the sources that I mentioned in Chapter 6, "How to Share Posts."

2. Copy the link of the article or blog post.

3. Grab a screenshot from the website source. If there isn't a picture that I like, I go to Wikipedia to find a picture. If there's nothing at Wikipedia, I sometimes buy a stock photo from Fotolia (http://us.fotolia.com/). I use Snapz Pro X (http://www.ambrosiasw.com /utilities/snapzprox/) to take the screenshot.

   If I'm embedding a YouTube video, I don't take a screenshot; I include YouTube's "share" link so that people can watch the video right in the post.

4. Compose the post in the entry area. The first part of my posts is the day of the week and the number of the post for that day—for example, "(Thu05)." I do this (and no one else on Google+ does) for two reasons: first, to keep track of the number of posts I shared so I don't do too many; second to make my followers aware that they missed some posts, so that they should go back to look for them.

   If my post contains a link to a website, Google+ grabs a photo from the website. I let it do this to test whether the link works even if I'm not going to use the picture—there's nothing worse than 1,800,000 close friends clicking on a broken link.

5. Remove the automatically included image and text from the website by clicking on the "X" on the right side of the text box.

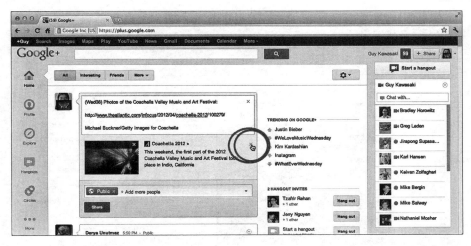

Removing the automatic image.

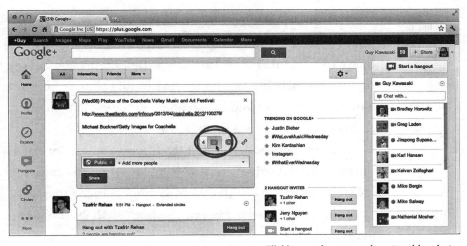

Clicking on the camera icon to add a photo.

6. Add a photo by using the gray (which turns blue) camera icon. I almost always replace the image that the link automatically delivers because the image often doesn't convey the essence, power, or beauty of the topic.

7. Click on "Public" to share the post.

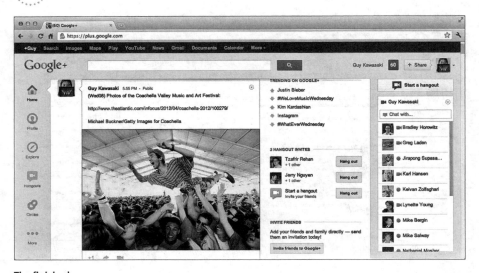

The finished post. This is why I like to manually add a picture to my posts.

The final post with my manually selected and added photo. During the hours of 8 p.m. and 8 a.m. Pacific, I use Do Share to schedule posts. This means that I don't control the picture as much, but I am willing to sacrifice the aesthetics of a post in order to avoid the spammy and insipid comments that occur when Southeast Asia is awake.

Also, my procedure is slightly different when I'm cruising the Internet using a phone or tablet. At these times, I'm looking for articles to share but not to compose that post. I use the Opera browser to scan sources such as Alltop and StumbleUpon.

I've set up a circle that contains only me as a member. When I find something good, I share it with only that circle. Later, when I'm back on my MacBook, I go to my profile to find the post, copy the link in it, write a new post, add a photo, share it, and delete the original post that I only shared with myself.

Few people use processes that are as long and convoluted as this, and I'm not recommending that you follow my example, but sharing on Google+ is an art form for me.

CONCLUSION

Google+ is a deep product—so deep that you could drown if you tried to master it all in a short time. As you gain familiarity with the service, try these advanced techniques. They will increase the utility and fun of Google+. And please pass along what you learn to others for the betterment of the entire community.

Additional Documentation on Google's Website

Google+ for Business

(http://www.google.com/+/business
/#utm_source=google&utm_medium=cpc&utm
_campaign=pages)

About Google+ for Mobile

(http://www.google.com/mobile/+/)

Google+ Pages Discussion Forum

(https://productforums.google.com
/forum/?hl=en#!forum/pages-discuss)

How to Evangelize Google+

> EVANGELIST, n. A bearer of good tidings, particularly (in a religious sense) such as assure us of our own salvation and the damnation of our neighbors.
>
> AMBROSE BIERCE

THINK DIFFERENT

Macintosh evangelists were the unsung heroes of Apple. Apple did not pay them, and most Macintosh evangelists were not shareholders. Their motivation was a love of Macintosh and a desire to help people become more creative and productive by using Apple's new computer. They provided support when Apple couldn't or wouldn't and helped keep Macintosh alive during the dark days of the late 1980s.

To evangelize Google+, or anything else, people need to help others "think different." In the case of Macintosh, potential Macintosh users had to think different rather than default to Windows. In the case of Google+, people need to think different rather than default to Facebook or Twitter.

In the course of trying to convince thousands of developers to write Macintosh software, I learned that the most effective way to evangelize something new is to demonstrate it. This chapter explains how to evangelize and demonstrate Google+.

DEMO DIFFERENT

I've demonstrated Google+ to hundreds of people, and these are the features of Google+ that have worked well for me:

- **Editing.** Show people that you can edit a post or a comment after the fact. You can't do this with Facebook and Twitter. You can do this with Pinterest, but few people compose long posts or comments on Pinterest so editing doesn't matter.

- **Customizing.** Reorder the icons in the navigation ribbon on the left side of the window. For example, move "Circles" above "Profile" by dragging and dropping. I don't know of any place on Facebook, Twitter, or Pinterest where you can customize the user interface this easily.

- **Ripples.** Select a post that's been shared at least 20 times (it doesn't have to be yours) and launch "View Ripples" to show the utter coolness of ripples. The easiest way to find a popular post is to click on the "Explore" button in the navigation ribbon on the left side of the window and peruse the "What's hot" area.

  While you're mentioning Ripples, you should discuss Facebook's Edgerank system where only 10 percent of your friends and family can see your updates. Roughly speaking if Facebook has 10 times more people but only 10 percent can see your updates, that puts it on par with Google+, right?

- **Google+ search.** Ask your audience what their passions are and do a search for the keywords in Google+—not a regular Google search but a Google+ search. Show people that almost every search yields people, posts, and circles. In other words, everyone can find people who share the same passions on Google+.

- **Circles.** Add a few people to an existing circle and show how to create a new circle. Explain that this is a way to organize people along parameters such as interests (knitting, hockey, etc.) and relationship (friends, family, colleagues, etc.). Also, demonstrate how to remove people from a circle.

- **Block and report.** Pick a post in your stream and show how easy it is to block and report a person for the unfortunate and infrequent instances when you want to get rid of a bozo. Other services can do this too, but you should at least help people check the "get rid of bozos" box.

- **Notification.** Show people the notifications you've gotten for +mentions and explain how useful it is to know when people have mentioned you anywhere in Google+. Other services can do this too, but Google+'s method is very elegant.

- **Creative Kit.** Click on one of your pictures in your posts, launch "Creative Kit" (upper left corner) and show people the built-in picture editor of Google+. It's very handy to have photo editing built into one's social-media service.

- **Social search.** Perform a search of a term that is relevant to your audience. For example, if you're with entrepreneurs, search for "venture capital" and show them how the results of a Google search now include the posts of people that you circled. (To make this work, you have to know that the people you follow have shared posts about the topic.)

Also, point out how the right sidebar provides suggestions of people to circle who write about the topic.

- **Hangouts.** Start a hangout to show how you and nine buddies can video conference. Point out how cool this is for communicating with family, friends, and customers. Then show a YouTube video of two guys that people might have heard of, the Dalai Lama and Desmond Tutu, sitting around and shooting the breeze.

I've added an "*" to the parts of this book that explain these features.

CONCLUSION

The word "evangelism" comes from a Greek word that means "good news." With this list of tips and ones that you perfect on your own, I hope that you'll go forth and spread the good news about Google+.

Afterword

This book has been a labor of love because I love to write, I love to help people, and I love G+. I want you to love Google+ as much as I wanted people to love Macintosh.

On Google+ you'll find a diverse group of intelligent, passionate, and engaging people who are moving and grooving in an elegant, feature-rich, and secure environment. If I help you derive greater value and pleasure from using it, then my job is done. And I try to never leave a job undone.

While it's never too late to start using a Macintosh or Google+, I hope this book encourages you to embrace Google+—to jump the chasm in one Michael Jordan–esque (or Jeremy Lin–esque) leap!

As Steve Jobs used to say, "There must be a better way," and in this case, there truly is. Let me know how things are going. You know you can +mention me 24/7/365, and I'll get back to you.

About the Author

Guy Kawasaki is the author of 11 books, including *Enchantment, Reality Check, The Art of the Start, Rules for Revolutionaries, How to Drive Your Competition Crazy, Selling the Dream,* and *The Macintosh Way.* He is also the cofounder of Alltop and a founding partner at Garage Technology Ventures. Previously, he was the chief evangelist of Apple. Kawasaki has a BA from Stanford University and an MBA from UCLA, as well as an honorary doctorate from Babson College.